Inventions, How To Protect, Sell And Buy Them; A Practical And Up-to-date Guide For Inventors And Patentees

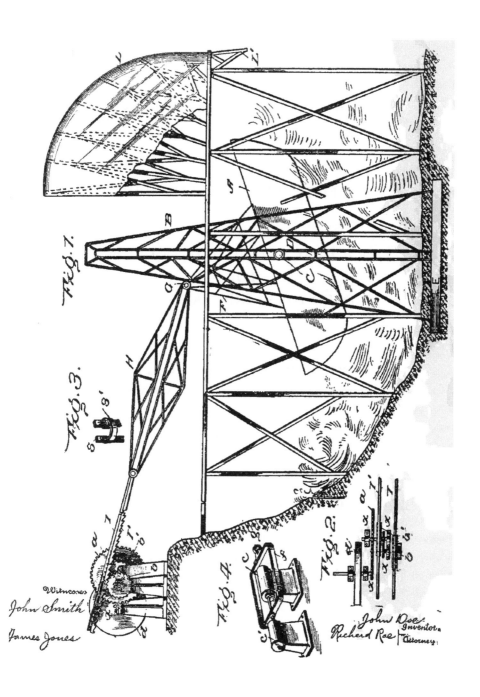

Fig. 1.

Fig. 3.

Fig. 2.

Fig. 4.

Witnesses
John Smith
James Jones

John Doe
Inventor.
Richard Roe
Attorney.

INVENTIONS

HOW TO

PROTECT, SELL AND BUY THEM

A

PRACTICAL AND UP-TO-DATE GUIDE
FOR
INVENTORS AND PATENTEES

BY

FREDERIC B. WRIGHT

ATTORNEY-AT-LAW, COUNSELLOR IN PATENT CAUSES

NEW YORK
SPON & CHAMBERLAIN, 123 LIBERTY STREET

LONDON
E. & F. N. SPON, LIMITED, 57 HAYMARKET, S.W.
1908.

Copyright, 1908
By Spon & Chamberlain

Press of McIlroy & Emmet, 22 Thames Street, New York City

PREFACE.

THIS book does not pretend to teach inventors how to be their own attorneys, nor how to prepare and prosecute an application for Patent. The time-worn adage that he who is his own lawyer has a fool for a client, is as true of patent law as it is of other branches.

It would be impossible even within the scope of a much larger volume to go into the details of patent practice. An attorney or solicitor becomes skillful in the drawing and prosecution of patent cases not so much from any reading of text books as by constant application of the law every day to concrete examples. It is not so much that he is learned in the fundamental principles which anyone may learn for himself as that he is learned and experienced in the application of these principles. Each case differs in detail from every other and what at first sight seems the most simple may turn out to be the most complex and subtle.

It may be asked then, why should the inventor bother himself with the law at all; why not leave every thing to his attorney? There are a num-

iii

ber of reasons. No inventor can properly instruct his attorney unless he understands the principle on which Patents are granted, and what a patent means. Again no patentee or owner of a patent right is in position to make his invention profitable unless he understands the rights and privileges conferred upon him under the grant. Again he cannot properly follow and understand the conduct of his case as it passes through the Patent Office. Further than this, he wastes time and energy in devising unpatentable or commercially impracticable mechanisms, or in taking out patents which are of no value.

Ordinarily, it is only after several experiences with patents that an inventor comes to understand what he is after and why he gets it, and it is to give him this information at the start that this book has been written. The Author believes that this book, small as it is, will be of value to every inventor whether he be a tyro with a wonderful first idea, or one who has been through the mill several times. The statements of the Law may be relied upon, and the suggestions as to how to invent, or dispose of the invention are the result of a considerable experience with inventions on the part of the writer both as an Examiner in the Patent Office at Washington and an Attorney practicing before it.

The Publishers will be pleased to answer any questions on the subject matter of this book.

CONTENTS

PAGE

Introduction I

CHAPTER I.

THE NATURAL RIGHTS OF INVENTION AND THE PUBLIC.

Monopolies and Patents. Patents in the United
States I

CHAPTER II.

THE BUSINESS OF INVENTING.

The Process of Inventing II

CHAPTER III.

THE NATURE OF A PATENT AND PATENTABILITY.

The Considerations of the Grant. Principles or
Systems not Patentable. An Art or Process. A Machine. A composition of matter. An article of Manufacture. What is not patentable. A principle of
nature. A manner or System 20

CHAPTER IV.

THE CONSIDERATIONS FOR WHICH A PATENT IS GRANTED. NOVELTY AND FULL DISCLOSURE.

The requirements under Novelty. Previous Patents
or use. A published description. Previous public
knowledge. Unpublished description. Unidentical devices as anticipations. Not patentable inventions.
The well-known proportions of a material. A substitution. Mere variations. Changes in the make leav-

v

PAGE

ing off or adding unaccentual parts. Double use, new
use. Mere aggregation of old elements. Public Use.
Inventor's Consent. Abandonment. What is public
use? Experimental use 28

CHAPTER V.

SOLE AND JOINT INVENTION AND JOINT OWNERSHIP.

When an invention is not joint. Employer and Employee. Invention made by Employee and ownership
thereof. Joint Ownership 38

CHAPTER VI.

PROTECTION BEFORE APPLYING FOR A PATENT.
CAVEATS.

The   application,   etc.   Attorney's.   Documents.
Claims. Specifications. A Caveat. Partition for a
Caveat. Reduction to Practice. Delay is not excused.
Lack of money 42

CHAPTER VII.

THE APPLICATION FOR PATENT AND ITS PREPARATION.

The Patent Office Procedure. Searches and free
examinations. The Application. The Claims. Filing.
Specification. Examination 56

CHAPTER VIII.

PATENT OFFICE PROCEDURE.   ·

Interference. Rival Inventors. Re-issues. Extensions. Marking Patented 84

CHAPTER IX.

TRANSFER OF PATENT RIGHTS.

Selling and Buying Patents and Right therein. As-
signments. Grants. Licenses. Recording. Agreements of all kinds 95

CHAPTER I.

THE NATURAL RIGHTS OF INVENTORS AND THE PUBLIC.

THE right to the product of a man's brain is not an inherent right. Originally society, that is others than the creator, recognized property right only in those objects which were tangible and visible and indeed only then when they were actually in the possession of their owner. The lump of clay molded into a rude bowl, the rounded stone pierced for the insertion of a handle and strapped into place with leather thongs, if laid aside became the property of him who picked it up and could defend his possession. Only very gradually as the evolution of society made it necessary did the idea of a right of property separate from possession take root and grow.

Before going into the details of the present *artificial* patent rights, it will be well to consider briefly an inventor's or discoverer's *natural* rights.

Naturally, man had no rights in an idea, once

I

the idea was given to the world. If he devised
a new form of flint arrowhead, he could keep a
monopoly of it, keep it exclusively to himself only
so long as the embodiment of that idea was not
seen by others of his tribe. Once seen by others
they were at perfect liberty to make their flint
arrowheads like the new one if they so chose.
The inventor reaped no profit from his invention
after his secret had been discovered and hence it
was to his advantage to keep the secret hid. Of
course, this was to the manifest disadvantage of
the tribe.

While secrecy was hard to keep in the case of
a tangible body like an arrowhead, we will suppose the case to be a new *method of making* arrowheads which the inventor might practice in the
privacy of his own cave or in the depths of the
forest. It would be to the tribal advantage to
learn the secret as it would give the tribe a greater
offensive and defensive capacity. It could only
learn the secret however, either by forcing the inventor to explain it or by rewarding him for his
disclosure. If it was not disclosed the inventor
might die or run away and his secret be lost or
carried to some other tribe. The tribe, therefore,
for its own protection would come to an agreement with the inventor whereby in exchange for
teaching this new art — this improved process —
to others, who could carry it on, he would be
given a lump return, or allowed to have a monop-

oly of practicing the art while he lived or during a term of years. This would set him up as the chief manufacturer of arrowheads in all the country round; a person of consequence, honors, and many cowrie shells.

This arrangement, it will be seen, would be in the nature of a compromise between the natural right of the tribe to use any improvement it saw fit once the idea had been shown to it, and the natural right of an inventor to withhold the secret of such an improvement if he could do so. Now it will be seen that the reward is not so much for the *inventive act* as for the *disclosure*. The reward is not for any inherent virtue in the inventor, not for his learning how to do the thing, but as payment for teaching his knowledge to the tribe or Nation. It is a plain business deal with consideration on both sides, and it is as a plain business deal with a tribe or nation through its head or government that we must conceive the whole matter of patent rights. Too many consider a patent right as a gift from the people, as a reward naturally due to an inventor for his smartness, as payment for the pains and labor required to invent. This is not the case. The payment is for the *disclosure* of the idea whereby the tribe or nation shall benefit. If it had been as a reward, the reward would have been equally due whether the thinker had disclosed his idea or not. He would have been just as ingenious and just

as clever in one case as in the other, but without
the disclosure the world at large would not have
benefited.   This doctrine of the benefit to the
community as a consideration for the granting of
exclusive rights is the key whereby the whole question of the mutual rights of the public and the
inventor or discoverer may be easily adjudicated.
The patent, as will be seen in a later chapter, is
merely a contract between the public on one side
and the inventor on the other, and it may be ended
by a failure of consideration like any other contract.

These principles have been very clearly put by
Mr. Robinson, in his exhaustive treatise on Patents,
wherein he says that the fundamental grounds on
which all patent rights rest are

> " I: That the inventor having made such an
> invention as is entitled to the patent privilege,
> must communicate it to the public by publish-
> ing an accurate description of its character and
> uses.
> II: That the public having received from
> the inventor this communication must thence-
> forth during the period for which his privi-
> lege is granted protect him in the exclusive
> use of the invention so described."

The reader will note that it is required, however,
that the inventor should have made " such an invention as is entitled to the patent privilege " in order
to give the consideration necessary to bind the

public in protecting him to the exclusion of others and that it is not any discovery on his part that so entitles him. A great many inventors believe that they are entitled to a reward for their work without regard to its being a disclosure to the public of something new or something old. They have the notion referred to above, that the inventive act itself is rewarded. A consideration of what has just been written on the subject will show them the mistaken nature of their ideas.

Before considering in detail this contract between the inventor and the Public, it will be well to distinguish between the ancient monopolies and Letters Patent for Inventions as we know them to-day.

The origin of the patent system in this country may be generally said to be found in the Royal Grants by which the sovereigns of England gave to an individual or a private or public company a monopoly in trade or manufacture, thereby granting the exclusive privilege of making or using or selling certain articles, which but for the grant any other person would have had a right to make, or use, or sell. In the olden times it was often necessary that such monopolies should be granted in order to encourage manufacturing or trading enterprises, and indeed an analogous grant may be seen in the exclusive rights of way and subsidies given to our early railroads. Without such large grants and assistance Capital could

never have been got to take the risk incident to
what was then a novel and uncertain enterprise.

If this had been the only reason for granting
monopolies all would have been well, but from
granting exclusive rights to common things on
grounds of public policy, and the encouragement
of arts and commerce, the rulers gradually slipped
into the habit of granting them for favors done
to the Crown — for money or services and eventually as a matter of mere favoritism.   Under these
circumstances, the commonest articles became the
subject of monopolies; salt, vinegar, starch, paper,
iron and many other necessaries of life could be
manufactured and sold only by a favored few.
These abuses became so excessive and burdensome
that eventually the power to grant monopolies of
common articles was abolished in the reign of
James I. of England.

Such monopolies as these, it will be seen, violate
the fundamental principle of their existence.
There was no consideration for the grant; the
property of the public was taken away and nothing was given in return.   In the case of a disclosure of a new art or manufacture, however,
nothing would be taken from the public by granting a monopoly, and this distinction was recognized by the " Statute against Monopolies," which
expressly excepted grants of exclusive privilege
made to inventors and discoverors of *new* arts or
manufacturers.   To these the Crown could grant

a monopoly of making or selling for a certain limited number of years in consideration of their disclosing the invention or discovery. This Statute is the source of the Patent Laws of the United States.

The principle of the Patent Law was a part of the common law which we received from England and was put into practice by the separate States even before any general United States Laws were passed. The foundation of the general Patent Laws, however, is to be found in the Eighth Section of the 1st Article of the Constitution where power is granted to Congress to . . . "promote the progress of Science and Useful Arts by securing for a limited time to authors and inventors the exclusive right to their Inventions and Discoveries."

Under this Act Congress has from time to time passed laws regulating the means whereby exclusive rights of this character may be acquired and determining the terms and conditions of the Grant. These laws have been changed and altered frequently, but of the specific changes made in the law by the Acts of 1793, 1794 and 1800, etc., etc., it is unnecessary to speak. Our business is with the Statutes as they stand to-day and of these the Revised Statutes 4886, 4887, and 4888 are the only ones which need to be considered. These are given below. In addition the reader may be referred, for an extended consideration of these changes, to the

volumes of Walker, Curtis and Robinson on the
Law of Patents.

"SEC. 4886. Any person who has invented
or discovered any new and useful art, machine,
manufacture, or composition of matter, or any
new and useful improvements thereof, not
known or used by others in this country, before his invention or discovery thereof, and
not patented or described in any printed publication in this or any foreign country, before
his invention or discovery thereof, or more
than two years prior to his application, and
not in public use or on sale in this country
for more than two years prior to his application, unless the same is proved to have been
abandoned, may, upon payment of the fees required by law, and other due proceeding had,
obtain a patent therefor.

"SEC. 4887. No person otherwise entitled
thereto shall be debarred from receiving a patent for his invention or discovery, nor shall
any patent be declared invalid by reason of
its having been first patented or caused to be
patented by the inventor or his legal representatives or assigns in a foreign country, unless the application for said foreign patent was
filed more than twelve months, in cases within
the provisions of section forty-eight hundred
and eighty-six of the Revised Statutes, and four
months in cases of designs, prior to the filing
of the application in this country, in which
case no patent shall be granted in this country.

"An application for patent for an invention or discovery or for a design filed in this
country by any person who has previously

regularly filed an application for a patent for the same invention, discovery, or design in a foreign country which, by treaty, convention, or law, affords similar privileges to citizens of the United States shall have the same force and effect as the same application would have if filed in this country on the date on which the application for patent for the same invention, discovery, or design was first filed in such foreign country, provided the application in this country is filed within twelve months in cases within the provisions of section forty-eight hundred and eighty-six of the Revised Statutes, and within four months in cases of designs, from the earliest date on which any such foreign application was filed. But no patent shall be granted on an application for patent for an invention or discovery or a design which had been patented or described in a printed publication in this or any foreign country more than two years before the date of the actual filing of the application in this country, or which had been in public use or on sale in this country for more than two years prior to such filing.

"SEC. 4888. Before any inventor or discoverer shall receive a patent for his invention or discovery, he shall make application therefor, in writing, to the Commissioner of Patents, and shall file in the Patent Office a written description of the same, and of the manner and process of making, constructing, compounding, and using it, in such full, clear, concise, and exact terms as to enable any person skilled in the art or science to which it appertains, or with which it is most nearly con-

nected, to make, construct, compound, and use
the same; and in case of a machine, he shall explain the principle thereof, and the best mode
in which he has contemplated applying that
principle, so as to distinguish it from other
inventions; and he shall particularly point out
and distinctly claim the part, improvement, or
combination which he claims as his invention
or discovery. The specification and claim
shall be signed by the inventor and attested by
two witnesses."

CHAPTER II.

The Business of Inventing.

The old recipe for jugged hare began with
" First catch your hare " and this rule is as appli-
cable to patents as it is to cookery. Indeed, inventions are much more elusive things than any
hare ever was. You cannot go out with a gun and
bag a patentable invention nor can you set a
trap for it, and this chapter which is written in
an endeavor to give a number of useful hints to
the inventor bids fair to be the hardest to write
of the whole volume. A recipe may be given for
the cookery of the hare, but none for the catching.

And yet from the author's experience it would
seem that would-be inventors, or rather would-be
investors and profit-takers, need some advice as to
the best application of their powers,— the best investment of their time and labor,— which in many
cases is time and labor thrown completely away.
The invention is made, the Patent procured, nicely
framed perhaps and hung up on the wall,— and
yet no profit comes from it to the great amazement
of the Patentee. Three chances out of five he
blames the Government or the purblind manufac-

turers, and denounces the Patent System, when it
is no fault but his own. He has forgotten that he
is merely an investor who has made a bad investment. He is oblivious of the fact that the Government cannot make the public buy what they do
not want. He overlooks his standing as a mere
purveyor and fancies that he should have a reward
for the act of inventing regardless of what he invents and how. If he will keep in mind that he is
in the same position as the vender of any other
commodity, he will not be so prone to fancy himself an ill-used individual, because the public de-
clines to buy his wares. The Government is no
more to blame for the unprofitableness of his invention than it would be if he had picked out and
taken up a homestead right in the expectation that
a big city would be built in the vicinity which should
increase the value of his property manifold and no
city had been built. It was a mistake on his part,
or a misfortune. As for the Public, let him place
himself in the position of the Public,— of one con-
templating buying the invention, if he can do so,—
and he will at once see the difficulties in his way.
Unfortunately, the majority of inventors are like
the majority of other creators; they believe the
children of their brain to be faultless and resent
the least suggestion of imperfection, hence the difficulty of any impartial, business-like and cold-
blooded view of their creation.

There are two elements in every invention: The

End to be attained and the Means whereby that end is attained. The end may be reached by a circuitous and involved path or by one running directly to the object. As a straight line is the shortest distance between two points, the direct method is always the best. Too many inventors fancy the attainment of the end by *any* means is sufficient. It is comparatively easy to get mechanism to produce an effect but it is difficult to devise the *best* mechanism for the purpose,— the simplest mechanism, the most direct-acting, the mechanically proper mechanism.

The casual, amateur inventor usually errs in this manner, and hence produces a mechanism of such a complication, of so many parts, so badly co-ordinated and combined that the machine is practically worthless. It is to this class of inventors that the world is indebted for Railway Gates, whose "sticks and strings" would never stand the first shock of operation, rotary engines that can never be pursuaded to make more than one revolution, folding beds that do not fold. These, too, are the inventors of churns, dish-washers, fire starters, music turners, lock nuts, non-refillable bottles, and a host of domestic appliances,— inventions conceived at the fireside and carried out with string, cardboard and wire. It is wonderful to see how these matters repeat themselves over and over in the Applications filed in the Patent Office, each time with an innocent belief in the absolute novelty of the means and an ignorance of anything like it having ever been devised worthy of Adam himself.

Inventors of this class, that is the casual and careless inventor with no training in mechanics, should be on their guard as much against the too-obvious way of getting over a difficulty as of the too complicated and round-about. If the way is so obvious, then why has it not occurred to some-one else? Probably it has, and some one else has tried it only to find it *practically* inoperable. When I speak of the obvious way I do not mean necessarily the simple and direct. Some of the most obvious combinations of mechanical elements to produce a given result are the most complicated. Inventive skill is shown in devising, through long study and experiment, a simpler and more direct means to the end. The rule should be: Select that which is the simplest possible means capable of *completely* attaining the required result.— Not an easy thing to do but the Public is not paying for the doing of easy and obvious things.

There is another error many amateur or casual inventors fall into. They invent useless things. Marvels of ingenuity, but ingenuity misplaced. Conglomerations of intricate mechanism for doing something which can be far more easily and quickly done by hand or in an entirely different manner. A machine capable at the cost of considerable time and trouble of writing letters in long hand, might be a very wonderful piece of mechanism but it would hardly be of value to the world if letters could be more simply and easily produced by the old fashioned method, or in a different manner by a typewriter. The casual amateur inventor, with only a slight knowledge of mechanics, does his best and most profitable work on some small object of daily use and need. Let him not tackle complicated problems. The Public is willing to pay for two things: Clever inspiration,— or dogged, continual, plodding hard work, based upon experience. The copper-toed shoe, the return ball, the Waterman pen clip,—these are examples of the first class. The Hoe press, the telephone, the turbine engine, the typewriter are examples of the second class.

There is another kind of casual inventor though who usually succeeds both practically and financially, oftentimes indeed making a fortune by some simple improvement. This is the practical worker in any special field. He cannot be called a professional inventor for he does not devote his time to this, but neither is he altogether an amateur for he has a practical working knowledge of the field in which his improvement lies. This is the man — or woman (though the latter usually invents by sudden inspiration) who devises those improvements on already existing machines which tend to increase the working capacity or to perfect their operation. These, through daily experience in a factory or shop are aware of a need or defect and are likewise aware of what has been done and of the conditions to be considered. These are the practical common-sense "smart" men, the ideal "Yankee" inventor and it is perhaps this class who make more by invention than any others.

It is the methodical and trained mechanical engineer of learning and experience that the world owes for the second class of inventions. These are not conceived one day and perfected the next. Men of this stamp take infinite pains with their work, neglect no effort at perfection and make themselves by long study and experiment, experts in their particular lines. These are professional inventors, and as they require no suggestions as to their procedure, this reference to them is sufficient.

The process of inventing. There can be no rule of course laid down for the production of sudden and clever inspirations. They come into the mind of man without warning and often without preceding conscious reasoning, but even as regards inspirational inventions the following suggestions may be made:

Be sure that the device suggested will do the work. Try it. Try it completely and under service conditions.

Consider carefully how it can *best* be made. When you have worked this problem out, go to a mechanic skilled in that particular art and get his suggestions. Should it be cast, or forged or stamped? Can it be made in a shaper or does it require hand work? Is it difficult and expensive to assemble? Have you combined and co-ordinated the individual elements and reduced the mechanism to its simplest form? When these questions and others are all answered,— then, and only then have you practically perfected your device and commenced reduction to practice.

How the invention is to be manufactured is one hardly ever considered by the amateur inventor, and too frequently lost sight of by men of experience. Yet it is most important and on it oftentimes depends success or failure.

Study carefully the actual working conditions of a trade or art if you are desirous of improving it; — the speed at which your machines must work to be commercially practical, the material they must handle, and its peculiar shape, consistency or texture. Consider also the finished product, whether defects therein will render it unsaleable or not. These are vital matters. The writer knows personally of a case where an invention was bought and some fifty thousands of the devices manufactured and put on the market. They met with a ready sale for apparently they filled a great need. Yet after a few weeks' trial they were returned on the hands of the manufacturer. They could not work certainly at the speed required, and for want

of certain assured action were of no value. The
Company failed and the inventor lost a large sum
in possible profit simply bcause of incomplete invention.

Case after case might be cited showing the necessity of working knowledge of the conditions of
operation and the inventor is warned to take special care in this regard.

Another example may be given along this line.
Some thousands of alleged non-refillable bottles
have been devised yet a very large per cent. of these
cannot be manufactured by glass workers, the parts
cannot be molded nor blown, nor can they be as-
sembled. Another cause of failure in this line is
the ignorance of most non-refillable bottle inventors as to the expert methods used in filling bottles.
The most expert maker of non-refillable bottles for
inventors stated to the writer that there was not
one bottle in a hundred which he made that he
could not easily refill by using one or another of
the many methods known to experts.

There is one other stumbling block of which a
certain class of inventors should be warned. Do
not take nature as a guide. Animals progress by
means of levers called legs, yet no one would ad-
vocate mechanical legs in place of wheels as a
means of propelling vehicles. A fish swims by
means of its tail, but the application of an analogous mechanism to the propulsion of vessels in
place of the screw-propeller, would be absurd.

Nature can suggest to the inventor, but always remember that machines and living creatures are different things. This advice might seem needless but for the weird schemes every now and then broached to a derisive world.

CHAPTER III.

The Nature of a Patent, and Patentability.

A Patent is usually considered to be a grant, in the nature of a gift to the inventor, a prize, awarded to him, as a prize of Five Dollars might be awarded at a County Fair for the fattest hog, or the largest pumpkin.

A Patent is not a prize in that sense, nor a reward, nor a gift. It is a contract, and nothing more.

Like any other contract, a patent is dependent upon the keeping of its conditions. The Patent Office, when it signs the contract by issuing a patent, does not agree to guarantee that the conditions, as far as the Patentee is concerned shall be fulfilled and remain so. It only guarantees that if the conditions are as claimed by the Patentee, then he shall be allowed certain artificial rights.

It is analogous to a Government grant of certain mining rights. A man sees what he believes are indications of gold. He investigates and decides that the gold is present in the rock. He alleges his belief, and claims the mining rights. The public through the Government grants him the right to mine that land,— in other words, to get gold from it — if gold is there. It does not guarantee him that gold *is* there, and if he fails to find any gold it is his own fault or misfortune and not the Government's.

The Public through its representatives, cannot guarantee either the value of a Letter Patent, nor can it guarantee that the conditions on which the contract or patent is based have been fulfilled by the Patentee. That is something for which he must look out himself. The Government's part is negative. It is up to the inventor to fulfil the conditions.

If a party agreed to buy everything new a seller produced, he would not be obliged to pay money to the seller unless the latter had produced something new. And if it could be shown that an article which was bought by the first party as new was not really new, the seller could not complain if he was required to repay the money wrongfully secured.

This is generally understood in transactions between man and man,— but it is not understood in transactions between a man and the Public. This is largely because the Government, i. e. the Patent Office is substituted for the Public,— and the Public is forgotten. From the earliest ages it has been considered right to get anything from the Government possible. There is reason in this view when the Government represents a power apart

from the People, when a grant or franchise is a
mere act of favoritism, but there is none where the
Government is the *Commonwealth,*— the Publ' ,
itself. It is not the abstraction called the Gover᾿ .
ment which is granting you something out of i ;
own treasure chest of privileges, but the Peop
of the United States who are giving to you a po᾿᾿
tion of rights otherwise theirs, and giving it ᾿ ᾿᾿
you for certain recognized and defined consider᾿᾿
tions.

A clear understanding of this is necessary. To ᾿᾿
many inventors fancy when their patent is broke ᾿
in the Courts and found invalid, that it is somehov ᾿
the fault of the Government; that the Public, hav
ing granted a patent should defend it from at᾿
tacks by itself, that the Government has guaran ᾿
teed the validity of the patent by issuing it. Thos᾿
inventors, usually have an appliance not wortl
patenting,— are full of grievances and are prone tᴄ
denounce the Government and the Patent Systen
as if they had been defrauded. They cannot bᴇ
defrauded of something they never had. They hac
a patent, yes, but the right of which the patent iⲟ
merely evidence they never had. They believed
they had it, the Patent Office believed they had it,
but as a matter of fact the Courts have decided that
they did not have it.

A United States Patent is a contract or agreement between an inventor and the people of the
United States, that assuming he has devised some

new thing, not before known, he shall be given an exclusive right to manufacture, use and sell the new device in the United States for a period of 17 years (or 7, 14 or 21 years in the case of Designs).

This agreement is based upon the disclosure to the Public of some new thing of value to it. If it is not new, then there can be no disclosure, for there is nothing to disclose. If it be of no value to the Public they do not care for the disclosure. We have therefore novelty and utility, as the conditions precedent to this contract. Novelty, requiring a large consideration will be taken up in the next chapter, but of utility it may be said that this requirement is purely negative. Any invention which is not deleterious to the physical or moral health of the Nation is held to be useful. Inventions for immoral purposes, gambling devices, etc., etc., are not " useful " and are not patentable.

A United States Patent is granted to anyone, whether a citizen of the United States or a subject of a foreign Government, whether man, woman, or child, who is the original inventor or discoverer of a new and useful thing or art, within the meaning of the law. A United States Patent is granted for the whole term of 17 years in the case of inventions in arts, machines, manufactures or compositions of matter, but not for any less period than the whole term.

Patents for mere ornamental inventions, called Design Patents, are granted for terms of 7 years,

14 years, or 21 years as the applicant may elect
when he files his application.

There are five great classes of inventions for
which patents may be granted: Arts, Machines,
Manufactures, Compositions of matter, and Improvements thereon.

An art or process may be defined as:

> A mode of treating certain materials con-
> sisting of a series of acts performed upon the
> material, which may make it better or trans-
> form it into a different thing.
>
> The acts performed may be either chemical
> or mechanical, and the result may be either a
> change in the chemical constitution of the prod-
> uct or its mechanical constitution.

All methods of preparing a product, whether the
product be bread, or iron, or building material or
textile fabric (to name some instances) are arts.

The novelty of the method consists either:

> In the production of a new material (in
> which case the novelty of the invention con-
> sists in the new use to which the old method
> is put)

or

> In the novelty of the steps themselves.
> Each step by itself need not be novel, though
> it of course, may be, but the combination of
> steps must be, and their relation to each other.

A machine may be defined as:

A combination of mechanical elements, or powers, so co-ordinated, and put together that when set in motion, they shall all act together to produce a certain predetermined physical effect.

While an art covers the steps or acts by which a result, without reference to specific mechanism, is procured, a machine covers the mechanism capable of carrying through a certain series of steps or acts. As a matter of fact the term mechanism or machine is so well understood that there is no necessity of considering this class further.

A composition of matter may be defined as:

An article or product composed of two or more substances, chemically or mechanically combined by chemical union or mechanical mixture. This product may be either a fluid, a powder or a solid.

An article of manufacture is so broad a term that for all practical purposes it may be said to include all inventions, not properly classed as machines, processes or compositions. On the one hand it covers small parts of machines, capable of being separately manufactured and sold; on the other, combinations of mechanically combined materials, not properly " compositions."

Thus, a stove lid or a paint brush would come within the term, as well as a textile fabric, a house or a street pavement.

The distinction between a machine and an article of manufacture lies in the fact that an article of manufacture is not capable of being set in motion and by its own operation attaining any predetermined result, while a machine is so capable.

What is not patentable. The non-patentability of an invention or discovery is very hard to set forth, and indeed may be best stated by reference to specific matters which are not patentable.

A principle of nature is not patentable, but only the means whereby the principle is applied. Thus a patent would not be granted on " using gravity as a means of delivering grain to vessels " on " sending signals by electricity," on " magnetism " or " on the use of steel where strength is required."

Thus the first discoverer of magnetism could not have an exclusive right to all applications of this principle. The discoverer of the fact that steel is hard could not patent this discovery and have an exclusive right to the use of steel in all situations wherever hardness was a requisite.

A process or art which is not useful is not patentable.

A manner or system of performing certain work which does not produce a product is not patentable. Thus a manner of playing a game is not patentable, though the appearance of the game, the

cards, pieces, boards, implements, etc., are. A
manner of plowing, or reaping, a manner of sewing, a manner of keeping books, a manner of getting the attention of the public or of exploiting
the sale of an article or of advertising, are all unpatentable. There is no tangible product and, assuming the means used to be old, nothing on which
a patent can be issued.

The above remarks also apply to a way or manner of packing goods, or displaying them before
the public. This may be a convenient way, an at-
tractive way, a profitable way, but if it does not produce a mechanical effect, or result in a new product,
it is not patentable.

Every Patent Attorney receives "inventions" of
this type on which an application for Patent is suggested, and hence it has seemed necessary to the
author to particularly describe what can not be the
subject of a patent in order that his readers may
be delivered from the mistaken, but general impression that a way of doing work, not properly an
art, is patentable.

CHAPTER IV.

The Considerations for Which a Patent is Granted:

NOVELTY AND FULL DISCLOSURE.

The requirements under " novelty."

> That the invention shall not have been known before conception.
> That it shall not be obvious.
> That it shall not have been given to the public after its invention.

The real requirement for a valid consideration on which a patent may be granted is that the invention shall not be already the property of the public. The Government has no more right to give the property of the public to one man than to appropriate the public money in the Treasury to a private use.

If an art, a machine, a manufacture, or a composition is known to the public, and used by them a sufficient length of time then the Government has no power to deprive the public of their property, and give the exclusive use, sale and manufacture over to a private person.

28

Previous patents or use. The most obvious case of an invention having been known before, is when the actual subject-matter has previously been patented, or even previously in common every day public use. If it is patented, the rights to it belong to the Patentee. If not patented the rights to it belong to the public.

A mere public *use* in a foreign country will not prevent the grant of a patent in the United States,

The reason is that such use, may not be known to citizens of the United States, and the law assumes that such a *foreign* use is not known unless evidence to the contrary is given.

A published description in a foreign country, is assumed to imply a knowledge in the United States because a published book or article is available as a source of information to citizens of the United States, and such *publication* would be a bar to the grant of a patent or render a patent invalid.

Previous public knowledge without use. Again, though never used, if the invention has been described and set forth in some volume to which the public has access, either in this or a foreign country, so that the public might have known if it chose, a patent can not be issued, as the invention of public property. The description however, must be so full and complete as to put the

public in full possession of all the facts necessary
to an operation of the invention. A hint or suggestion of possibilities will not do.

Unpublished description. A *prior application*
for patent is not an anticipation, for as it has never
been published, it is not publicly known and is
therefore assumed not to be the common property
of the Nation.

A mere written description, not published for
common circulation, not placed where the public
may read, and learn, is not such public knowledge
as will anticipate an invention, or render a patent
invalid.

Unidentical devices as anticipations. What
constitutes the quality called "invention." What
are obvious changes.

Anticipation by prior devices, or matters which
are identical with the supposedly new invention, is
easily understood, but anticipation by reason of
unidentical things is very rarely understood by the
ordinary inventor, though it forms the subject of
the larger part of the decisions of the Patent
Office and the Courts.

The line dividing false "invention" or non-
"invention" from true invention is very hard to
distinguish, and in this debatable border land between them, you will find the highest authorities
differing. Just so you will find the highest author-

ities differing regarding the beauty of a picture, or
the literary value of a book.

**The following matters are not " patentable in-
vention."** A mere change in the proportions of
an old device is not patentable. To make a thing
larger or smaller; to make its parts relatively larger
or smaller, is within the rights of anyone. This
manner of adapting the apparatus to varying conditions of work, is considered to be plainly obvious. Thus changes in the proportion of gears
to increase or decrease the speed of a machine,
changes in size fitting it to an analogous use, do
not involve invention,

Substituting one old and well known material
for another, is not invention, but a mere obvious
change. Such a change may be good and the device so made may be better adapted to its work,
and be more commercially valuable, but it is obvious. It is well within the general knowledge of
the public, and the right to make such a change
cannot be given to one man to the exclusion of another.

The well known properties of a material are
within public knowledge, and the use of that common knowledge is public property. Where one
man used iron, another seeing that the iron rusted,
cannot get a patent on using brass or copper, for
the non-corrodible properties of these metals are

well known.   There must be some new effect gained
from the substitution; an effect not before known
to exist.

**A substitution of one old and well known
form of gear** or mechanical movement for another is considered obvious.   Certain combinations of wheels and levers to produce a certain, effect are well known to any mechanic, and
their use is public property.   One form may possibly work better than another, but the selection of
one form rather than another is merely a matter
of good judgment.   It does not rise to the dignity
of a creative effort and should not be rewarded specially.

Mere variations in form, not accompanied by
or giving rise to changes in actual result are obvious.   These may tend to cheapening the cost of
making a device, as by cutting down on the amount
of material need, or the amount of work required.
and are therefore commercially valuable, but they
are not patentable.

Changes is the manner of making a device,
when one old process or manner is used for another, are not patentable.   If a device, or part of
an apparatus has been heretofore forged it is obvious to cast it instead.   If a shell has been heretofore spun, it is "obvious" to make it by stamp-
ing.

Leaving off, or adding unessential parts is obvious when no essentially different result is obtained.

Double Use.   It may be said that :—

To use an old device in a manner which is analogous to its use before, is considered obvious, where the results produced in the two cases are analogous. Thus, the use of a joint in the tubing of oil-wells, would be analogous to the previous use of such a joint in gas pipes. The use of a peculiar form of clutch in a dental drill, would be entirely analogous to the use of the same form of clutch in rock drills. A blower for blowing grain along a tubular conveyor would be analogous to the use of a rotary fan for forcing water through a pipe. The use of packing rings in the piston of a steam engine would be analogous to the use of the same rings in a pump piston.

The test of double use is:— Do the two like devices operate in the same manner to produce a like effect. If they do, one is not patentable over the other.

New use.   When two devices are similar in construction, but their operation is different and their effect is different, the use of the device in a new situation is not obvious, and is patentable " invention." In such cases as this it has required a certain cleverness and genius to see the new use.

It is not the construction which has been invented so much as the use itself.

The screw was well known ages ago. Its principle was thoroughly understood. It was used for raising water. The screw was fixed and the water moved. Nevertheless the use of a screw on a ship acting against the water, the screw moving with the ship and against the water was a new use, not obvious, and entirely patentable.

Mere aggregation of old elements, in one construction is obvious, and not patentable. This may be illustrated by imagining an automobile of ordinary type, but composed of elements old separately, but never before all brought together. The lamp we will suppose to be old, the horn old, the steering mechanism the same as used in another machine, the transmission gear of no novelty, the tires of a common type, the pump old and well known, etc., etc. There would be no invention in aggregating all these old elements on one body. The total would be merely the sum of each element taken separately. It might be a very fine machine. It might be most convenient to have all these separate devices on the same machine, but the law would consider such an agglomeration as obvious, and as much within the rights of the public as wearing a red cravat with a black coat and gray trousers, or requiring as little invention as hanging a pencil to one end of a chain, and a watch to the other.

The inventor and the buyer of inventions should in this matter consult a patent attorney who is skilled in applying the decisions of the courts, and the rules of the law.   It is but rarely that any other than a professional inventor or patent lawyer is capable of distinguishing what is " invention " over what is not, and indeed even the professional inventor is not to be trusted.   The invention is his child, and he is prejudiced in its favor.

Public use.   While if an invention is known or used by others before the inventor's conception, it is of course public property, let us suppose that after the inventor's conception but before his application for Patent, it became known to others.

Knowledge, without a use prior to the application, has no effect as a bar to the patent, but if the invention was *in use,* or *on sale* in the United States for *more than two years,* before the inventor applies for his patent, such use is a bar to the grant, and renders a granted patent invalid.

Consent of the inventor is not necessary, as far as the public at large is concerned, though if it could be shown that the idea of the invention was stolen from the inventor, then it is probable that this lack of consent or knowledge on the inventor's part might be considered.

In the first case, however, the matter is and has become public property, because of an independ-

ent invention by some one else, but the Use and
Sale Clause of the Statute refers not to the Public's acts, but to the inventor's negligence, and the
oath taken by the inventor that the invention has
not been in use or on sale for two years prior to an
application, is simply that he has not deliberately
abandoned it.

Abandonment may be either tacit or deliberate.
If the inventor does not perfect his conception and
reduce it to practice he is considered to have abandoned it deliberately.

If he allows others to use and manufacture it,
for two years prior to perfecting his rights, he abandons it.

If he drops his experimenting, does nothing further with his construction until some one else re-
invents it, it is abandonment. If he lets his application lapse for non-payment of fees, he abandons
it.

In other words, he either drops his work, thereby
doing nothing for the public for which he should
be paid, or else he gives his invention to the public,
and cannot retake his gift.

The inventor must remember that: —

Any actual sale or use — no matter how slight
is Public Use and Sale, and if occurring two years
before the application is an absolute bar to the
grant.

Any gift by him of the machine or article or process, etc., is a public use.

Allowing another to make the device, or to use the same, is Public Use. It has even been held that when a corset attachment was worn by one person alone with the inventor's permission for two years before the application was filed the attachment being concealed, yet such use was " public," and rendered the subsequent patent void.

The inventor must beware of two things, generosity and negligence, if he wishes to protect his rights.

What is not public use under the statute. The law presumes that the inventor must have time to experiment and perfect his invention and opportunity for doing so.

Experimental use is therefore not considered public, even though carried on in public, for there are many inventions which cannot be tried out in any other way. Such are inventions which have to be tested on public conveyances, or put up where the public can handle them. Such use should be limited to experiments, solely,— and either no profit derived or the profit is entirely incidental.

CHAPTER V.

Sole and Joint Invention and Joint Ownership.

The laws provide that Patents shall issue to original *inventors,* their representatives or assigns. There is no other manner in which Patent can be granted in the United States,— though, in foreign countries the introducer of an invention may procure the patent in his own name. Notwithstanding this, this matter of who shall apply for a patent on an invention is one very little heeded by inventors. If you want your patent to be void, one of the surest ways is to have it granted to you and another who is not an inventor.

When only one person devises an invention it must be applied for by that person only.

When two or more invent, the application must be made by all the inventors.

It makes no difference that a sole inventor is willing to share his invention with another, or that several inventors are willing to give their rights to one; the patent must be applied for by the inventor or inventors. If you wish to transfer your rights to one man, or to several, do so by assignment, as explained later.

When an invention is not joint.   Putting up money to finance an invention, or assist the inventor does not constitute the friend an *inventor,* but merely a partner.

When two persons each invent distinct and operatively separable parts of a device, they are not joint inventors.   They must each take out a separate patent.

When one merely suggests the need or usefulness of a device, without suggesting any means, he is not a joint inventor with him who devised the construction itself and reduces it to practice.

Employer and employee.   When one devises a construction, but employs another to make the device and reduce the invention to practice, there is no joinder of invention.   An inventor has a right to employ the skill of others to perfect his invention, and suggestions made by such employee, or improvements so adopted belong to the original conceiver, and not to the employer, nor is the employer a joint inventor.

Invention made by employer, and ownership thereof.   When one is employed to make an invention, and does so in fulfillment of the contract, the invention belongs to the employer, though the application for patent must be signed by his employee.

When an invention is made by an employee, not
under a specific direction, and in the employer's
time, it belongs to the employee entirely.

If a machine is made or a process devised, and
another is allowed to construct and use the machine
or operate the process, without objection, then the
inventor is barred or estopped from claiming any
income or pay for that machine or use. The invention is of course the inventor's, but the user
has been given what practically amounts to a license.

Joint ownership. Joint inventors, or assignees
of a patent are " tenants in common." They each
have an undivided share.

They are partners and hence the act of one is
binding on all. One of the owners can grant a
license — contract for royalties, make or release
agreements just as well as another, or the whole of
them can, and this does not matter whether he has
an undivided one-hundredth part, or an undivided
three-fourths interest.

Each of the several joint owners can make and
sell and license others to make and sell the invention, without regard to the other owners and without regard to the amount of his undivided interest.

Hence it follows that when it is desired to keep
or acquire the control of an invention, a company be
formed, in which the controller shall have the majority of shares of stock. To this company the in-

ventor assigns his invention out and out. He can thus keep the control or sell it as he desires.

There is much misunderstanding about this matter of joint ownership — and inventors and buyers of patents should remember the foregoing in all transactions.

CHAPTER VI.

Protection Before Applying for a Patent.
Caveats.

THE inventor cannot be too strongly advised to
keep records of the growth of his invention, not
only as a means of refreshing his memory and that
of others to whom the invention in its various
stages was shown, but also as evidence to be used
either in Interference proceedings or in Infringement suits.

He should note the date of his conception of the
invention.

He should preserve his first rude sketches noting
the date when made.

He should preserve his first models in such condition that they may be identified by him and by
his friends, and if possible in such condition that
their operation may be self-evident.

Bills for work done in connection with the experimental period, letters referring to his progress,
old diaries, photographs made from time to time,
all these may become of great value in proving
the dates of conception, experiment and reduction
to practice.

It is not necessary that every scrap of this sort

should be kept, but only that he should have a consecutive record of the work done, so preserved as to be easily produced and identified.

The following plan is a good way of identifying and fixing the date of conception. Let the inventor make a clear sketch of the salient features of his mechanism or device and write out a brief but clear description of it. Attach to these the following attestation of a Notary or Justice of the Peace and have him impress his seal upon *all* the papers through the attestation.

County of ⎫ ss:
State of ⎭

On this   day of   personally appeared before me, John Doe, a Notary in and for the county and State aforesaid, Richard Roe, to me personally known, who made oath that the papers hereto attached contain a description and drawing of an invention conceived by him on the   day of   of which he believes himself to be the original and sole inventor.

(Signed) JOHN DOE,

(Seal.)   Notary Public.

To this attestation might be attached others, as of a confidential friend, to the following effect:

State of ⎫ ss:
County of ⎭

John Robinson, being duly sworn, deposes and says that he is personally acquainted with

Richard Roe, that on the   day of   he
was shown the drawing and description hereto
attached and knows that the said Richard Roe
claims to be the inventor of the construction
therein set forth.

(Signed) JOHN ROBINSON.

Sworn to before me this   day of
(Seal)   JOHN DOE,

Notary Public.

The impressure of the seal should, if possible, be
visible in *all* the papers as thus they are identified
as having been attached to each other and as being
the papers referred to in the attestation.

It will be seen that there is no need of the
Notary seeing the contents of the papers if this is
not desired. He is simply attesting the date of the
papers and the claim of the inventor. If he sees
them, however, and understands the invention, so
much the better as he can thereby be so much a
better witness if a witness is needed.

It will be seen that a paper such as this is much
stronger evidence as to the date than a paper merely
signed and dated by the inventor himself. The inventor might have fraudulently ante-dated a paper
of this kind but it is not likely that he could have
procured a Notary of Justice to misdate it for him.

While caution should of course be used in showing an invention to others, yet it must be also borne
in mind that by showing and describing the device

to others the date of the inventive act is more certainly proved than by the unsupported testimony of the inventor alone.. It is well as a matter of record and as a means of fixing the date of such disclosure that these others should sign a memorandum or swear to a statement that they have had the invention described to them on such and such a date,— the statement identifying the invention as clearly as possible, either by reference to its effects or its construction. The latter is preferable.

Remember that vague and uncertain testimony is of little value and hence that the better your witness knows the invention the more valuable his testimony will be.

This is well illustrated by the testimony presented by Daniel Drawbaugh in the famous Telephone cases, which though great in volume was so vague as to be of hardly any value as proof. Drawbaugh alleged that he invented the telephone some years prior to Bell, and in support of this allegation he produced fragments of old models and apparatus and some hundreds of witnesses to testify that they had known of his invention years prior to Bell's conception.

The " models " merely consisted of *disjecta membra,*— of fragments gathered from the scrap heap, not capable in themselves to show that they were parts of an operative electric telephone.

The witnesses testified vaguely that they understood that Drawbaugh had invented a means of

transmitting speech,— that they had heard Drawbaugh talk over some sort of a transmitting mechanism, but not one of them could tell what the mechanism was or how it was alleged to operate, or if
it operated electrically at all.   As far as their evidence went the mechanism might have been a speak-
ing tube or a string telephone.   The Supreme
Court decided that Drawbaugh had not proved his
case,— at least as against conclusions to be drawn
from certain inconsistencies in his actions, and
awarded priority to Bell.

This case illustrates the danger of being too ret-
icent, too secretive, but there is equal danger in being too frank.   A hint of an invention even may
be the means of starting another man on the trail,
and either bringing a device into public use (see
Chapter IX) at a date sufficient to defeat the inventor's right or permitting the other man to procure
a valid patent through his earlier reduction to practice and more diligent action.

And here is another caution: Do not present
your friends with specimens of your invention as
gifts or sell it to them unless you intend to apply for
your patent immediately, as such gift to a friend,
more than two years prior to the date of the application, has been held to be sufficient public use to
defeat a patent.

A Caveat.   Beyond taking the precautions above
described, there are no other means whereby an in-

ventor can protect his rights during the period of experimental work, except by filing a Caveat in the Patent Office.

A Caveat is a notice or warning to the officials of the Patent Office that you are working on a certain idea, trying to bring it to that stage of perfection whereat it may be patented. A Caveat merely lays your claim before the Patent Office and entitles you to be warned of the filing of an application by someone else for a patent on like subject matter.

A Caveat is good for one year. It may be renewed however, at the expiration of its time by the payment of another fee. If during this time an application is filed by another party for a like construction the Caveator is notified of this fact and also notified that he must file a regular application for patent himself within a reasonable time. If he does so, the two applications are placed in " Interference." If he does not do so, he is held to have abandoned his case and the Patent issue to the applicant.

If the invention is so far perfected that it is operative, and complete, do not file a Caveat unless forced to do so by lack of means. It is a waste of money for the regular application has still to be filed and it does not give near the protection that the application does.

As a Caveat is for an incomplete invention and as it is merely a warning to the Patent Office it may be very informally prepared. It consists of a Petition, Description, Oath and Drawing.

The Petition is as follows:

Petition for a Caveat.

To the Commissioner of Patents:

Your petitioner,   , a citizen of the United States and a resident of   , in the county of   , and State of   , (or subject, etc.) whose post-office address is represents:

That he has made certain improvements in and that he is now engaged in making experiments for the purpose of perfecting the same, preparatory to applying for letters patent therefor. He therefore prays that the subjoined description of his invention may be filed as a caveat in the confidential archives of the Patent Office.

Signed at   , in the county of and State of   , this   day of   , 19 .

. . . .

Attached to this is the description beginning as follows:

To all whom it may concern:

Be it known that I, John Doe, have invented certain new and useful implements in   of which the following is a description.

This should be clear and as exact as possible but need not have any formal claims.

Accompanying the description is the following oath

State of
County of   } ss:

John Smith, being duly sworn deposes and says that he is a citizen of the United States and a resident of   County of   , and State of   ; and that he verily believes himself to be the original, first and sole inventor of the improvement in   herein described.

(sig.).

Sworn and subscribed before me, a Notary Public in and for the County of   , State of   , this   day of   ,   .

The drawing may be a mere sketch, a drawing on tracing cloth, or a blueprint, but it should show the construction as clearly as possible.

The Government fee on filing a Caveat is $10. If possible the Caveat papers should be prepared by an attorney, though the necessity of an attorney is not as important as in preparing an application.

Reduction to practice.— Delay in filing application. The inventive act does not end with the conception of the invention. That conception may be vague or it may be extremely definite and clear, but if the inventor rests upon his oars at this stage he is liable to lose his rights entirely. Either the public will acquire these rights or some inventor, possibly independent, possibly a rival with knowledge of his invention, will by the exercise of superior diligence acquire the rights.

As was stated in Chapter I, the law does not contemplate rewarding an inventor for doing nothing. It does not reward the inventor, as has before been stated, for merely inventing, no matter how much of a mental effort that act may have been or what ingenuity, care, experiment or expense was involved. A mere idea lying in the inventor's brain does the country no good. The inventor might die, he might depart for a foreign country and nothing be ever heard of his invention again. Unembodied inventions are never in a form which is entirely practical. When an invention is transferred from the inventor's brain or from paper to the workshop it is usually found to be inoperative as first devised. It requires to be worked out, to be brought down to a practical basis and numerous modifications must be made before the machine is an actual operative commercial device. Until the construction is on this basis the inventor is not considered to have accomplished anything worthy of reward.

The inventive act is not ended by merely making a drawing of the machine. It continues throughout the whole period of experiment and only ends with the final reduction to practice.

Reduction to practice does not mean the mere making of a model. It means the making of a machine of such size and such construction as will operate under service conditions. It does not mean a mere experimental device of sticks and strings and cardboard and tin, nor even an elaborate and costly model on a small scale. It means a working device; a device capable of showing the accomplishment and fulfillment of the inventor's ends, capable of being tested under service conditions, capable of showing its operativeness and value under these conditions. This is the second stage or it may be termed the third stage in the inventor's journey, the first stage being conception, the second stage the preparation of drawings and models, the third stage being actual reduction to practice. Then and then only has the inventive period terminated.

Applying for a Patent. Many inventors do not wait for complete reduction to practice before applying for patent, but if the device is reduced to practice first, the inventor should apply for his patent as soon as possible thereafter. He need not wait to absolutely perfect the construction if the principle is so clearly correct that no great changes need take place in order to fit it to actual use. Every day's delay weakens his right to patent and can be excused with difficulty. The courts do not look with favor upon delay and negligence and it takes strong proof to convince the court that the delay was unavoidable.

Delay is not excused by the desire of the inventor to see if the invention will pay commercially. The inventor must take a chance. The cost of patenting is relatively small, smaller than the prime cost in other investments, and if the inventor waits for others to exploit his invention, and show that the device is of value thinking that later he will come into the game, claim the construction as his own invention and get the profit therefrom, he is mistaken. The Courts will hold that he should have the courage of his convictions and that he should have tried to protect himself and that if he did not do so he cannot reap the reward of other men's endeavors.

Business considerations are no reason for delay. The mere fact that you cannot come to an agreement with a manufacturing company, that you have a partner from whom you wish to break away, that you are waiting until you can make a change in your business relations,— none of these things are excuses in the eyes of the law.

Lack of money may be an excuse but it must be shown that this lack was absolute and actual. The fact that you could not afford to file the application will not be taken as an excuse. It must be actual inability; and the circumstances of the case, your own actions and the implications arising therefrom will be considered in this connection. If you have filed other applications but not *the* one, negligence will certainly be imputed. If it can be shown that you have made other investments and not this investment, you will be deemed to have thought very little of your invention. If you allow others to manufacture and use and say no word, delaying meanwhile the steps which you should take for your protection, the inference is that you had no intention of protecting.

The surest road for an inventor to take for loss of an invention is the Delay, Linger and Wait road. Once your application is filed and on record, you may rest upon your oars provided there is no rival inventor in the field, but if there is a rival inventor even after your patent is issued and he can show that he has been more diligent than you have, that he reduced to practice sooner, that he put it out on public use and sale sooner, even though he may have filed his application later than your application is filed, the patent will be granted to him and your patent will be void or your application rejected.

A prior conceiver will lose his rights as against a later conceiver but a first reducer to practice. A prior conceiver and first reducer to practice may lose his rights against a later inventor and later reducer to practice if the later reducer has put the device into public use and on sale earlier than the first reducer and has in other ways either protected his rights or given the device to the public.

Remember it is this disclosure to the public, this

advantage to the public which forms the foundation for all reward and that the country is not paying for or giving exclusive privileges as a reward to a man for inventing. It is for giving the invention to the public, giving the public something new and worth while.

To recapitulate, the inventor is advised to prepare drawings of his inventions, descriptions of the same, and to keep such drawings, to keep all important models, to keep records of his experiments and lists of those to whom he has shown the device. He is counselled to reduce to practice at the earliest possible moment and to file his application either before the final reduction to practice or as soon after as possible. He is advised indeed not to wait until his invention is absolutely perfect before filing his application. File the application on a broad idea and leave the details for a later application. The first application can be kept alive in the Patent Office but not issued until the second application is filed. This costs a little more but it is the best practice. Bell's telephone was not the perfect construction it is to-day when Bell's first application was filed. A telephone constructed according to Bell's first application would be almost inoperative, so crude is the mechanism and it was many years before the invention there embodied was brought to any commercial perfection.

Remember that while the patent is not given to

a first applicant irrevocably, and that even though you are a later applicant for the same device you can defeat the first application or even a patent already granted, yet that it is far better to have your application on file first, or have your patent granted first and thereby show by the record your diligence and your faith in the utility and value of your device.

CHAPTER VII.

The Application for Patent and its Preparation.

It is in the preparation of the application papers that the assistance of an attorney is almost absolutely requisite, for on the proper preparation of the specification and claims depends very largely the value of the patent. There are simple cases which may be prepared by the applicant himself and there are many cases filed in the Patent Office by an inventor without the assistance of an attorney, but the inventor is most earnestly advised not to trust to his own ability in this regard. There are very few inventors who really understand the proper preparation of a case, very few inventors who really understand the scope of a patent and almost none of them have more than a rudimentary idea of the manner in which a case should be prosecuted and argued. Very often an inventor will start the case himself, prepare the application and file it, possibly carry through one or two actions and arguments but before he has gone very far he finds himself in a bog of misunderstanding and either gives up entirely or seeks the assistance of one who is skilled in this particular form of practice and to whom the actions of the Patent Office are entirely clear.

The Patent Office endeavors as far as it possibly can to protect the interests of the inventor where the inventor is his own attorney but it is not the business of the Office to do this and it must be perfectly obvious that the employees of a great Government Department, overburdened with work, cannot give to one single inventor such assistance as he really needs. They will casually suggest to him certain changes or even tell him specifically how to amend the claims, but the author has hardly ever known a case where the inventor did not sooner or later retain the services of an attorney. And this must be borne in mind: That an application once filed cannot be changed so far as adding anything to the subject matter or taking away anything from the subject matter. The specification may be amended to more closely conform to the drawings or to better state the function of the invention or its operation, but it cannot be made to include what was not originally set forth. The statement cannot be varied in essentials: Hence if an applicant so states his case that the invention is not completely set forth, and important parts and essential elements are left out, he is bound by that statement and either must accept a patent which is defective for that reason, or else must abandon his case and

file a new one which would be quite as expensive
to him as procuring the services of an attorney.

It must be remembered that the Patent Office
uses a certain technical language. This language
is perfectly clear to patent attorneys but it is
largely a foreign tongue to an inventor unless he
has had a long experience.

Though the services of an attorney are absolutely requisite yet the inventor should himself
share in the labor of presenting his case. The
most skillful man cannot make bricks without straw
and unless the inventor assists the attorney by all
means in his power the specification and claims
may be defective. It is the inventor's invention,
not the attorney's. The inventor supposedly
knows more about it than any other person and
he should state his knowledge in full to the attorney and give him all the help he possibly can. He
cannot blame an attorney for defective patent if
he, the inventor, has not done his share. The inventor should disclose to the attorney all the facts
of his invention. The construction of it, the manner in which it may be manufactured if he knows
such a manner, and particularly the advantages
residing in it. He should, if possible, compare
it with what he knows to be the state of the art.
He should point out to the attorney the defects
of prior constructions and the way these defects
have been overcome by his own device or art.
The inventor should not assume that the attorney

is familiar with the mechanical side of the proposition. He may be or he may not. If he is, he will tell the inventor so and the inventor can very easily check up this knowledge by considering the work which the attorney does. But it is wrong to expect that an attorney will be necessarily fully acquainted with all the details of all the various arts and manufactures. It is true that his experience is usually a very wide one but it is not specialized as is the inventor's experience. The inventor should provide the facts as a party to a lawsuit does. It is for the attorney to take these facts and apply the law to them, to marshal these facts and display them before the Patent Office, to reason from them, and looking ahead to foresee future contingencies and to provide against them.

Don't go to your attorney with a mere nebulous and vague invention. Remember that his time is valuable and when you consult him have a clear drawing of the device ready to show him. Be clear in your understanding of it and try to explain every point.

Don't assume that you are the sole person in the entire world who has ever thought of this device. Most inventors become indignant upon the mere suggestion that there has ever been anything like their construction and when the attorney tells them that he hardly believes the device to be new, they look upon it as more or less of an insult and

suggest that in that case, as the attorney has no
faith in them, they will carry the case to another
lawyer. Thereby they are apt to lose the services
of an honest man and take the services of a man
who is perfectly willing to pretend to a belief in
the invention for the sake of the fees. Remember
that the attorney is rather apt to be cynical in
patent matters. He has had hundreds or thousands of cases presented to him, the larger portion of which are not novel in any sense of the
word. Hence he is liable to doubt the novelty of
almost anything presented to him unless the same
is particularly striking and effective. Many times,
too, an invention while really novel is so very
much like what has gone before that it requires
considerable explanation in order to show the difference between the old and the new. Don't spare
this explanation. Point out the distinction to the
attorney. Thereby he will be able to prepare your
case far better than he could otherwise do.

Another important point is to be sure that the
attorney does understand the case. Remember
that you are paying him for this understanding
and see that you get it. When the specification
has been prepared read it carefully. See that it
states your case precisely as you wish it and if it
does not do so, find out the reason from your attorney. If he shows you that as a matter of law
his statement is correct, it is best to bow to his decision, but on matters of fact your own judgment

is probably as good as his.   Many valuable claims
have been lost by the inventor being ignorantly
satisfied with an attorney's statement, the attorney being ignorantly unaware that the statement
is not sufficient.

Searches and pre-examinations.   Previous to
preparing the application it is sometimes advisable
to have a search made through the records of the
Patent Office to discover if the device or art is
novel and therefore patentable.   Where the invention is a simple one, an article of manufacture,
an uncomplicated combination of mechanical elements or where it is desired to discover whether
anything producing the same effect has ever been
patented, a search is most desirable.

Where the invention is complicated or one which
belongs to a class of mechanisms which has been
much worked over by inventors, a search does not
give very much information that can be relied
upon.   Many mechanisms are of such character that
the Patent Office drawings of them are very hard
to read and inventions in merely parts of these constructions are very difficult to search for.   In classes
of this character, a search is never by any means
certain and hardly worth while to attempt.   It is
much better to file the application with as broad
claims as you or your attorney think desirable and
then wait for the judgment of the Patent Office.
Remember that the judgment of your attorney on

these facts can never be final. You may believe in the novelty of your invention, and your attorney may so believe, but if the Examiner in charge of the class of devices does not believe in its novelty, you will either have to abandon the case or appeal it. If the Commissioner to whom you appeal does not believe in the novelty of the invention you will have to either abandon or appeal, and hence it follows that the opinion of the attorney based upon the facts as he finds them in the records, is not final. It is merely the opinion of an expert and you have no right to blame the attorney, at least in many cases, if his opinion is reversed by the Patent Office. There are always two sides to every law case and it is notorious that doctors, even the most expert, disagree in their diagnoses.

The application. After the preliminary examination has been made and carefully considered it next becomes necessary to prepare the application papers.

The application for patent comprises a formal petition; a specification or description of the invention with a full statement of its mode of operation, the claims wherein the specific points of the invention are pointed out; the drawing which shall show one or more embodiments of the construction, and the oath stating that the applicant believes himself to have fulfilled the requirements of the Statute.

The form of petition is to be found at the end of this chapter. The petition, as will be noted, should give the Post Office address of applicant and appoint an attorney to represent him before the Patent Office.

The specification and claims are the important points of the application. The specification is a description of the invention in such full, clear, exact and precise terms as will be understandable by anyone skilled in the art and as will disclose to the public the inventor's discovery and permit the public to carry on the discovery even were the inventor not alive.

Here again the inventor will see that it is the disclosure which is valuable, and that unless that disclosure is full and complete the inventor is giving nothing to the public, and if he gives nothing to the public the patent is of course invalid for lack of consideration.

The specification should not contain unnecessary description. Parts which are old and well known, of whose construction any mechanic is aware, need not be described at length, but let the inventor be careful that his specification whether prepared by himself or by his attorney points out and clearly sets forth the essential principles of his invention before the application is filed. If you believe that a point is not clear, call your attorney's attention to it. If you believe that a feature is not properly shown and described, call your attorney's attention to it. An inventor is entitled to the full aid and advice of his attorney and if the specification does not seem to him correct, he should not hesitate to bring it to the attention of his attorney.

It is sometimes necessary in order that the scope of the invention shall be fully understood that the specification shall refer to prior inventions or to the state of the art, pointing out the advantages due to the construction set forth in the application. Such references, however, should be in very general terms and should under no circumstances refer specifically to the patent of a rival inventor or to a rival construction. Statements derogatory of other inventions and invidious distinctions will not be allowed.

At the same time while the Patent Office will not allow such statements to be printed, it is oftentimes good practice to state them in the first instance in order that they may come to the attention of the Examiner so that he may see precisely what the applicant is driving at and note the distinction between the old and the new construction. Such statements as these and statements of advantages show the Examiner *why* a patent should be granted and an applicant must never forget that the Examiner should be shown why. It is the inventor's and attorney's business to show him why. The advantage accruing is the reason for the issue of the patent and unless some advantage does follow from the use of the invention then there is no ground for the issue of the patent.

In its formal features the specification comprises a statement of applicant's name, address and the title of the invention. Then follows a statement of the general class to which the invention belongs and the specific devices to which it relates. After this usually comes the description of the several figures of the drawing and then follows a description of the invention itself as illustrated in the drawings, the various parts being referred to by numerals or letters corresponding to the characters on the drawing itself. The specification usually winds up with the mode of operation of the invention, the manner in which it may be applied and the advantages to be derived from it.

Where there are equivalent elements or constructions which might be used without departing from the spirit of the invention, these equivalents should be stated, not necessarily specifically but in such manner that there shall be no misunderstanding with regard to the scope of the invention. If a part may be reversed, or two parts interchanged, this capability of reversal or interchangement should be stated. Remember that the claims are to be " read " upon the specification,— that they are to be construed by the specification, and that it is only through the specification that they can be properly applied. Remember also that the specification is meant for the world at large and

that if you do not fully explain your invention the
world will not understand it.

Defective specifications have often invalidated a
patent where the description was not so full and
complete as would make the invention understandable. Sometimes, where this defect has un-
intentionally occurred, it may be corrected in a
Re-issue, but where the defect or concealment is
fraudulent and for the purpose of misleading the
public, the patent will be absolutely invalid.

Inventors have sometimes fancied that it would
be particularly clever if they did not give to the
public the whole of their invention, if they retained
some important element in their own mind so that
after the lapse of seventeen years when the patent
had expired they would be still able to control the
trade. If the invention cannot be worked by
means of the information contained in the patent,
the patent is invalid. This cannot be reiterated
too strongly. Again the inventor will see why it
is so necessary that he give full information to
his attorney and if he does not give this full information he can only blame himself for defects
in the specification.

The claims are the heart and vital center of a
patent. Most inventors who have not had previous experience believe that the claims are statements of advantage and in writing to their attorney they are very likely to say:

" I claim, 1: That my invention is far superior to all others in simplicity. 2: That operating a harvester reel through an auxiliary lever on a rock shaft is far better than any other method heretofore devised, etc., etc."

These are not claims. They are statements of advantages and very poor statements of advantages at that. They have no part, in the crude form in which they are stated, in a patent specification.

The claims are specific averments of the boundaries of applicant's patent and they bear the same relation to the patent itself as the statement of boundaries, direction lines, etc., to be found in a deed. Everyone knows how particularly a deed has to be drawn and the same or even greater particularity has to be used with inventions. The function of the claims is to point out to the public precisely what the applicant believes to be his own. It is by the claims that the public is to guide its actions. If the applicant does not claim enough the public has a right to use what he has omitted to claim. If he claims too much the public's rights are just that much limited and curtailed.

There are two general forms of claims: Broad claims and limited or narrow claims.

The broad claim is in general very much more valuable than a narrow claim can possibly be. In the accompanying specification the broad claims have been marked with the letter A on the side, the narrow or specific claims with the letter C, and claims which are neither particularly broad nor particularly narrow have been marked B. It will be seen from a consideration of the broad claims that they are drawn to cover first the spirit of the invention in its largest application, and secondly the *essential* elements of the invention leaving out all reference to those incidents or incidental variations in form which are non-essential. Every non-essential statement which is made in a claim is just that much unnecessary limitation and detracts just that much from the value of the claim.

Reduce your invention to the simplest elements capable of complete operation. Cut out any reference to matters which do not tend to this unitary complete operation and the statement of the elements remaining will be a broad statement of your invention. If these elements are stated in terms of their operation the claim will be still broader and hence more valuable. Claims merely upon the function of a machine, its mode of operation as distinguished from its mechanism are not allowable, but claims which define a mechanism by reference to its manner of operation are allowable. It is almost impossible to so state this that the average inventor will understand it but it is not the aim of this book to make of the inventor a patent lawyer. It is the author's object to supply the inventor with such information that he will have some understanding of the efforts of the attorney and that he will be able to give to him just the aid which is necessary for a proper presentation of the case. Ignorance on the part of the inventor increases the attorney's work to a very large degree and may often render it nugatory.

Inventors are very apt to consider that a claim which states every item of a machine, or every step in the process, or every detail of an article of manufacture is particularly valuable. They will read such a claim which amounts to a catalogue of parts, will metaphorically smack their lips over it and insist that such claim is the one that pleases them best, utterly oblivious of the fact that such a catalogic claim as this is far less valuable than the simpler claims merely stating in general terms the construction of the machine. If the Government offered you the privilege of choosing any land within the boundaries of the United States, giving you the right to do with that land as you pleased, would it not be far more valuable to you than a grant of land, the land being set off by metes and bounds, the exact courses particularized, and every land-mark stated. In one case you have a free and unlimited choice of any parcel of land within a certain territory,— in the second case you are absolutely limited and bound by the courses laid down in your deed, and no choice is allowed you.

The claims of a patent are precisely of the same character. A limited, narrow or specific claim is one which lays down your allotment or right by

metes and bounds, hard and fast lines which you
cannot overstep,— whereas broad, simple claims
such as the claims " A " in the typical specification
following this chapter, give the inventor room in
which to turn, allow for variation, allow for the
principle of the invention being embodied in various forms and are made with reference to the
future and the many changes which may be desired.
If a claim states " a lever " for instance, the inventor may use any form of lever he desires without reference to its shape or to its class, but if a
claim states a bell-crank lever or a lever of a certain limited form, as for instance having a bifur-
cated end or being pivoted in a certain manner, the
patent is limited to thereto and any departure
from it avoids the claim.   Thus if the claim is limited as above, and another uses a different form of
lever or uses a lever in a different manner, or leaves
off the lever entirely, he is not within the terms of
the claim and cannot be held for infringement.   It
has been decided time after time that the dropping
of any one of the elements named in a combination
claim (that is, a limited claim where every element is named) will avoid infringement.   Thus
if a claim calls for combination of elements 1, 2,
3, 4, 5, 6, 7, etc., a manufacturer who leaves out
any one of the elements and only uses the elements
1, 2, 3, 5, 6, and 7 is not infringing the claim, the
element 4 being dropped.   It is to the inventor's
advantage then that the claim should only state

those elements which are *absolutely necessary* to produce a single result and to state such mechanisms only in general terms. If a certain combination of elements is absolutely necessary then every manufacturer will be obliged to use them, either alone or combined with other parts, but whether they are alone or whether they are combined with other parts, the person who uses this simple combination of elements must pay for such use.

It may be supposed from what has been said before that a patent without broad claims would be of no value and offers no protection to the inventor. This, however, is not the case. The value of narrow claims depends very largely upon the state of the art. If it has been much worked over it is impossible to get broad claims and the narrow claims may cover those perfections of the broad idea which tend to make the device commercially valuable, or to make it more valuable than slightly inferior constructions. If the inventor has a device which contains the final word in a line of invention, which perfects that invention and puts it in shape for better operation or quicker sale, the limited claim which recites the details of the invention will be practically as valuable to him as a broad patent.

The function of narrow claims is as follows: In case the broad claims are decided to be invalid by a court, the inventor can then fall back upon his narrow claims. It is like a series of earthworks, one behind the other. If the first defense is carried by the enemy, the defender can retreat to the second earthwork. If that is carried, then to the third and so on. That is precisely the value of limited claims. The broad claim might be found to disclose no invention and to be therefore invalid, but the limited claims including as they do a larger number of parts in the combination or a more detailed statement of construction, might retain their validity and cover the infringing device so fully as to gain the decision.

Remember that the claims cover a *mechanism, an embodied idea.* To merely conceive that it might be a good thing if a machine could be invented for a certain purpose does not constitute invention, and hence the Patent Office will not allow patents which are so broad as to cover all ways of performing a certain act. It is quite common after the grant of a patent for inventors to complain that others are doing the same work but with a different machine and ask "If anyone has the right to use any other machine than ours for that work." These parties may be the first to devise a machine capable of doing the work but they cannot merely because of that fact, prevent all others from inventing machines which will do the same work. Patents are not granted on merely doing work by machinery where it was before done by hand. They are granted for specific and concrete machines operating in a certain manner and capable of performing certain functions or for specific steps in a process. Hence if other parties devise a construction or process which is entirely different in principle and operation from your own construction or process they have a right to patent it and a right to use it without infringing your patent. The question is always as to how far they have departed from the construction; how far they have used the principles devised by you.

The drawings for the Patent Office are required to conform to very rigid requisites, as below. Models are not required by the Patent Office and will not be received unless they are specially requested by the Examiner.

The paper must be pure white, and of a thickness corresponding to three-sheet Bristol board; the surface must be calendered and smooth.

The sheet must be exactly 10 by 15 inches. If more illustrations are needed several sheets must be used. One inch from its edges a single marginal line is to be drawn, leaving the "sight" precisely 8 by 13 inches. A space of not less than $1\frac{1}{4}$ inch from the top within the marginal line is to be left blank, for the heading of title, name, number, and date.

All work and signatures must be within the marginal lines.

The drawing must be executed in deep black lines, to give distinctness to the print, and must be made with the pen only.

India ink alone must be used.

In shading, the same ink must be used, how-

ever fine the lines. Brush shading and pale,
ashy tints must be entirely avoided.

Letters and figures of reference must never
appear upon shaded surfaces.

Drawings should be rolled for transmission
to the office, not folded.

When views are longer than the width of
the sheet, the sheet is to be turned on its side,
and the heading will be placed at the right,
and the signatures at the left, occupying the
same space and position as in the upright
views, and being horizontal when the sheet is
held in an upright position; and all views on
the same sheet must stand in the same direction."

After your attorney has prepared the application
you should examine it and examine it most carefully. See that the description is correct and bear
in mind what has been stated with regard to the
claims. See that they are correct. Limited, narrow claims may be comparatively easily procured
from the Patent Office and attorneys who do work
at a very cheap price cannot possibly afford the
time and care necessary to prepare and prosecute
proper broad claims. Narrow claims are comparatively easy to draw. They may be almost laid
out by rule, but broad claims requiring as they do
an analysis of the construction in hand and a careful distinction between what is essential and what
is non-essential require time and thought, and a
large amount of work. If your attorney has not
seemed to grasp your idea, tell him so. Point out

to him that you believe he has not grasped it and wherein you think he has erred. If you do not understand the claims have him explain them to you. Have him explain their scope and the various equivalent constructions which any one claim might cover, and only after you are fully satisfied should you sign the application.

Only one invention may form the subject of one application, and this rule holds true even where inventions work together for one general end. The combination so formed must co-act,— one element with another. The mere fact that the two things may be used together, that it is convenient that they should be so, would not make them one invention. The rules of the Patent Office in this regard are very strict and where in the opinion of the Examiner an application covers two constructions a division is required,— that is, that claims to one of the inventions shall be cancelled from that case and either abandoned or filed in another case.

SPECIFICATION.

To all whom it may concern:

Be it known that I, JOHN DOE, a citizen of the United States, residing at Chicago, in the county of Cook and State of Illinois, have invented a certain new and useful Wave-Power, of which the following is a specification.

My invention relates to wave-motors and to

means whereby the intermittent energy of the waves may be transformed into a constant source of power.

One object of the invention is to furnish an economical, efficient, and easily-erected device by which the action of the waves may be rendered available by being transformed into other forms of energy.

A further object of the invention is to provide means for protecting that part of the apparatus exposed to the waves from submergence or undue violence of the waves. Generally stated, the invention embodies a suitable support and a float mounted in relation to said support and free to follow each phase of wave activity, whereby, through the media of suitable transmitting apparatus, to store up energy in the form of compressed air, electricity, &c.

The invention further embodies a suitable support, a centrally-pivoted float free to rock and reciprocate in said support to accord with varying conditions of wave activity and height of tide, means for converting the motion of the float into other forms of energy, and means for protecting the float from submergence or undue violence of the waves.

The invention further consists in certain novel constructions, combinations, and arrangements of parts hereinafter referred to and finally claimed.

The nature, characteristic features, and scope of the invention will be readily understood from the following description, taken in connection with the frontispiece, forming a part hereof, wherein —

Figure 1 is a side elevational view of a wave-power embodying features of the invention. Fig. 2 is a top view of the translating mechanism. Fig. 3 is a detail illustrating a means of uniting the supporting-girders. Fig. 4 is a perspective view of an air-compressor (shown as an example) whose piston-carrying frame may be attached to the transmission-rod.

Referring to the drawings, A represents the float, here illustrated in the form of a boat, held in place by the standard B, consisting of suitable supporting-girders S, secured together by means of metal straps S'. The float is provided centrally with pivots C, which are free to move vertically in suitable ways D of the standard or support.

E represents the foundation of the standard, here shown as embedded in the sea-bottom.

F is a framework attached to and moving on a universal joint G for operating through the transmission-rod H the translating mechanism located on the shore or on a float adjacent to the wave-motor. In the form herein illustrated for utilizing the power, I I' are two rods forming a fork on the end of the transmission-rod H and provided with teeth cut opposite to each other.

b b' are ratchet-wheels engaged by the teeth on I I'.

x x represent intermediate gearing for communicating the motion of the rods I I' to the power-wheel d.

c c' are two cylinders of an air-compressor, the piston-frame of which is attached by the joint g to the transmission-rod H.

L represents a protecting breakwater or wave-shield. Said shield may or may not be mounted on the standard or support B. In either event it is so located as to stand in the path of the waves acting upon the float A and so arranged that any wave of unusual size or violence will impinge against the shield and its violence or continuity be broken before reaching the oscillating float.

The operation may be described as follows: The float and its standard being located where there is a constant wave action, the motion of the waves causes the float A to rock up and down on its pivot C — in other words, giving it a bodily movement vertically and an endwise movement vertically. This rocking motion of the float is communicated, through the universal joint G, as a reciprocating motion to the transmission-rod H, to which are attached the oppositely-toothed rods I I'. The latter engage with the ratchet-wheels b b', and by means of the gears x x impart motion to the power-wheel d. The arrangement of the oppositely-toothed rods I I' with relation to the ratchet-wheels b b' is such that when the float rocks one way the teeth on rod I' engage and turn the ratchet-wheel b, and when it rocks the other way the teeth on rod

I' engage with the ratchet-wheel b'. The intermediate gears are so connected that a uniformly-directed motion of the power-wheel d results. As the tide rises and falls the float moves up and down in the slot or way D; but the parts are so arranged that at any angle of the transmission-rod H the teeth I and I' engage with the ratchet-wheels $b\ b'$. As mentioned above, the air-compressor $c\ c'$ can be substituted for the transforming mechanism of Figs. 1 and 2 by simply attaching the piston-frame f to the rod H.

It is not necessary that the transforming mechanism be located on the shore, as it may be located on the standard supporting the float or on a structure adjacent thereto. The centrally-rocking float may even be attached to an anchored float. The compressed air or the electricity generated or stored may be transmitted to the place of consumption by tubes or wires.

It is understood that the shield L may be located either on the same structure as the float or adjacent thereto. The lower portion L' of the shield projects downward such a distance as to be about the same level as the top of the float A when the latter is at its position of maximum activity. This downward projection L' will help to split and break up any unusually violent wave.

It will be obvious to those skilled in the art to which the invention relates that modifications may be made in details without departing from the spirit and scope of the same. Hence I do not limit myself to the precise construction and arrangement of parts hereinabove referred to, and illustrated in the accompanying drawings.

Having described the nature and objects of the invention, what I claim as new, and desire to secure by Letters Patent, is —

(A) 1. In a wave-motor, a float having a bodily vertical movement and an endwise vertical movement, means for converting such movements of the float into other forms of energy, and means for protecting the float from submergence or unusual violence of the waves, substantially as specified.

(A) 2. The combination of an oscillating float, means coacting with the float for converting its movements into other forms of energy, and means for protecting the float from submergence or unusual violence of the waves, substantially as specified.

(A) 3. The combination of a support, a float disposed relatively to said support and having a reciprocatory and a rocking movement, means coacting with the float for converting its movements into other forms of energy, and means for protecting the float from submergence or unusual violence of the waves, substantially as specified.

(A) 4. The combination of a support, a float having a bodily vertical movement and an endwise vertical movement, means for converting such movements of the float into other forms of energy, and a shield or breakwater mounted on the support and adapted to protect the float from submergence or unusual violence of the waves, substantially as specified.

(A) 5. The combination of a support provided with ways, a float having pivotal bearings adapted to said ways, the arrangement being such that the float is free to rock and otherwise follow the rising and falling motion of the waves, means coacting with said float for converting its movements into other forms of energy, and a shield or breakwater mounted on the support and adapted to protect the float from submergence or unusual violence of the waves, substantially as specified.

(A) 6. In an apparatus for utilizing wave or tidal power, the combination of an oscillating float, and a shield or breakwater adapted to protect the same from submergence or unusual violence of the water, substantially as specified.

(B) 7. The combination of a centrally-rocking float, a standard for said float, means for transforming the rocking motion of the float into rectilinear motion, a pair of oppositely-toothed rods engaging with corresponding ratchet-wheels, and intermediate gears for insuring a uniformly-directed circular motion, substantially as specified.

(B) 8. In a wave power, a vertical standard carrying vertical guideways, a float having trunnions entering said guideways, a pair of oppositely toothed rods connected to said float and engaging with corresponding ratchet wheels, and intermediate gears for insuring a uniformly directed circular motion.

(C) 9.   In a wave power, a vertical standard having oppositely vertical guideways, a float carried in said standard and between the guideways, said float being pivoted on trunnions projecting into said guideways and freely movable vertically in the same, an extension on said float projecting upward at right angles to the axis of the float, a pair of oppositely toothed rods, one end pivoted to said extension, a pair of ratchet wheels adapted to engage each with one of the toothed rods, and intermediate gears for insuring a uniformly directed and circular motion.

(C) 10.   In a wave power, a vertical standard having opposite vertical guideways, a float carried in said standard and between the guideways, said float being pivoted on trunnions projecting into said guideways and freely movable vertically in the same, an extension on said float projecting upward at right angles to the axis of the float, a pair of oppositely toothed rods, one end pivoted to said extension, a pair of ratchet wheels adapted to be engaged each with one of the toothed rods, a shaft on which said wheels are mounted, a main gear mounted on said shaft, a pinion with which said main gear engages, and a fly wheel rotating therewith.

In testimony whereof I have hereunto signed my name.

JOHN DOE.

In presence of —
JOHN JONES,
WALTER SMITH.

The above specification is copied from the specification of a patent now alive. The narrow claims, however, have been added to it and the name of the patentee and date of patent are changed. This is simply an illustrative specification.

CHAPTER VIII.

PATENT OFFICE PROCEDURE.

AFTER the application is fully prepared and signed it is forwarded to the Patent Office at Washington where it is filed. The fee payable to the Government upon the filing of the application is $15. This fee is supposed to pay for the work done in examining a patent. It does pay for small cases but it is far less than should be required in large cases. However, the Government makes no distinction between a complicated case and a simple one. The filing fee is precisely the same in all cases. When filed, the application is given a temporary number and a date for purposes of identification and the papers are placed in the "Secret archives" of the Patent Office until in its regular turn it comes up for examination.

No one can see this application except the officials of the Patent Office. You cannot find out if anyone has filed an application nor can your attorney. You will receive no information from the Patent Office in this regard. During the time that the application papers are being examined and until the issue of the patent the matter is kept entirely secret and no chance is given for attorneys or applicants to see the papers of other applicants.

There are some forty odd divisions of the Examining force of the Patent Office. Each device is in charge of a Primary Examiner and a large number of assistant Examiners. Each division has charge of all cases belonging to certain classes of invention, one division having for instance all classes relating to civil engineering works such as bridges, sewerage systems, building construction, the laying out of railroads, the cutting of tunnels, etc., etc., while another division will have all cases relating to internal combustion engines and their adjunctive mechanisms or elements.

After the application is filed it is sent to one or another of these divisions and in its turn is taken up for examination. It is usually at least a month and a half, and it may be six months before the case can be taken up for examination for the reason that the Patent Office force is insufficient and the number of cases filed in the Patent Office constantly increasing.

On the consideration of the case the Examiner in charge of it investigates thoroughly the state of the art by looking through the records of the Patent Office and also through the classified foreign patents, particularly the English, French and German patents. If he discovers that there is nothing like the invention, that it is a novel and not an obvious one, he allows the case and a notice of this allowance is sent to the applicant or his attorney.

It is very rarely, however, that an invention is totally novel at least as regards all of its claims. The invention may be novel, but the claims be so broadly stated as to include devices or principles already patented and hence the Examiner will object to such claims or reject them, pointing out to the applicant the reasons for this rejection and citing previously granted patents or other references. Many times these references do not appear to be anything like the applicant's device and the applicant waxes exceeding wroth in consequence, believing the Patent Office does not know what it is about. This arises largely from ignorance on the part of the applicant. It is not the specific invention which the Examiner is rejecting but the *claim* which claim may be so broad as to include within its terms devices of a widely different character.

Under these circumstances, let the applicant have a clear understanding with his attorney as to the pertinency of the citation made. Let the attorney explain to the applicant precisely why the claim is so broad as to include the device cited, then let the inventor point out to the attorney the differences which exist in construction, operation and advantages between the old device and the new. Many constructions which are apparently similar on their faces are found to be essentially different because of some apparently minor variation whose effect, however, completely changes the operation of the machine or its adaptibility to certain purposes.

Practical knowledge will enable the inventor to point out to the attorney matters in which the cited invention fails, things in which it is deficient or in-effective, things in which it is possibly inoperative or things which make it impractical from a commercial standpoint. It may be that the old device cannot be manufactured. It may be that the old device is not adapted to practical use. It is the inventor who should know this, not the attorney, and it lies with the inventor to point out to the attorney these facts so that he may properly amend the case.

The application may be amended as many times as necessary. This amendment cannot change the case in the sense of changing the construction described but it can change the case as far as changing the scope of the claims, cutting out and adding new claims and amending claims so as to more fully distinguish between the new and the old. There may be one action in a case. There may be a dozen. There may be fifty. The case may be allowed by the Patent Office within two months after it is filed or it may linger on for six or eight years. This depends entirely upon the novelty of the invention or upon its being understood by the Patent Office authorities. Finally, however, the patent will be either allowed or finally rejected. If finally rejected, the rejection can only be overcome by a favorable decision on appeal to the Board of Exam-

iners-in-Chief, to the Commissioner or to the Court
of Appeals of the District of Columbia. If allowed, however, as before stated, a notice is sent
to applicant.

This notice states the fact that the final fee of
Twenty Dollars must be paid within six months
after the date of the notice. The non-payment of
this final fee causes the application to lapse or for-
feit and to become abandoned. The application
can, however, be revived after forfeiture by the payment of a new first fee of $15. The case will then
be sent to the Primary Examiner to be again examined and again allowed. After the payment of the
final fee there is a period of a month during which
the case is in preparation before grant of the patent. During this time the specification is printed
and lithographed and reproductions of the drawings
are made. Upon issue the grant itself will contain
this printed description and reproduction of the
drawing as well as the formal deed or grant proper.
Once the patent has been granted the inventor
comes into his rights. He is then able to prosecute
infringers and to prevent others from using his device without paying him royalty or license fees.
He may keep it himself, he may transfer it to
others, he may form a company for its exploita-
tion. For seventeen years thereafter he is free to
make money out of it if he can and to prevent all
others from using, making or selling his device
without his consent.

The manner of handling a patent, however, or preventing infringement and of getting the most from the rights thus given to the patentee, must form the subject of another book. The subject is too large to be taken up in this volume.

Interference — Rival inventors. We have heretofore considered a case where an application for patent passes through the Patent Office with no objection except from the Examiner as to novelty, but just as the application may be rejected upon lack of novelty, so it may be held up for a determination as to whether the applicant is the original inventor or not.

This usually occurs where two applications covering the same subject matter are filed in the Patent Office at the same time by different inventors. Where this occurs, these applications are placed in Interference, as it is called. That is, they are sent to a special Examiner who has power to consider the testimony of the rivals as to priority of invention, reduction to practice and their respective record dates, and to decide from the evidence so presented to him who is the original inventor. When a case is placed in Interference both parties are notified of the fact, but neither party is told the filing date or number of the other party. They are required upon the receipt of this notice to file a preliminary statement under oath, this statement giving the date of conception, the date of making the first model or drawing, and the date of the reduction to practice. The dates given in the preliminary statement are binding upon the parties thereafter, and they cannot in later evidence seek to show that the conception or reduction was earlier than the dates made in the statement. Hence it is necessary that the statement be prepared with great care and exactness and that its dates be not matter of guesswork. Look back over your records or bills and receipts, letters, signed and dated drawings, and see precisely what the date is and thus when evidence is taken there will be no vital variance between the preliminary statement and the testimony which would prevent the testimony being accepted.

The Author does not propose to go into the various details of an Interference case. It is a matter which cannot possibly be handled without an attorney. It is a matter which must be very carefully handled. The rules of evidence are precisely those of a Court of Law and the testimony must be presented with as good an effect as possible. The testimony, by the way, is usually taken before a Notary and the testimony filed in Washington. Hence there is very rarely any necessity of the applicant himself appearing before the Interference Examiner.

The winning or losing of an Interference case depends upon the ability of the applicant to prove that he was the first inventor or the first reducer or the first applicant, and that he has in every way guarded his rights, that he has in no way been negligent of his interests, or that the opposite party was either a later conceiver, reducer or was so negligent of his interests as to have no rights to a patent. The question between two inventors usually resolves itself into a race of diligence and the party who has first given to the nation the fruits of his invention is ordinarily the one to whom the profits and rewards of the invention are given.

An Interference may take place at any time. It may be between two pending applications. It may be between an application and a patent. Or it may be between two patents on the request of the parties. Any number of applications may be included in one Interference provided they all claim substantially the same thing, and sometimes as in the great Telephone cases this Interference proceedings will drag on for years and the testimony will amount to hundreds of volumes. Such cases as these, however, are extremely rare luckily as an Interference is not by any means a cheap pastime. Witnesses have to be paid. The lawyers and Notaries have to be paid. The testimony and briefs have to be printed, and the inventor will thus see that he should weigh his chances very carefully before fighting through an Interference. The ordinary inventor, however, need not be worried as to this eventuality. Interference proceedings are comparatively rare, and by far the greater proportion of the applications go though the Patent Office without the slightest difficulty of this sort.

Re-issues. After the patent is issued, if there is found to be a defect in it, the patent may be re-issued and the defect thus cured. The difficulties which are curable by re-issue are such as render the patent

> " inoperative or invalid by reason of a defective or insufficient specification, or by reason of the patentee claiming as his own invention more than he had a right to claim as new, if the error has arisen by inadvertence, accident, or mistake and without any fraudulent or deceptive intention."

In these cases, and these cases only, is a re-issue ever granted.

The fee for a re-issue is $30, unless the Patent Office itself is responsible for the error, as where an inventor's name is wrongly spelled and some portion of the specification has been accidently left out in printing. Where the applicant or his attorney has been negligent of his rights and proper claims were not made, a re-issue will not be granted. Nothing can be changed from the original specification or drawing by re-issue unless to cure some inoperativeness. What was originally shown and described must remain the basis of the invention on which all new claims must be based.

Extensions. There is a popular impression to the effect that the patent may be extended beyond its term of seventeen years as a matter of course, or at any rate that the extension may be granted by the Patent Office on a proper showing. This is not the case. At one time extensions were so granted, though the matter of procuring them was one of extreme difficulty. To-day however an extension can only be granted by a special Act of Congress and is only given where the invention has proved of great public value and the inventor's reward has been entirely inadequate.

Marking patented. Prior to the grant of a patent the inventor may, if he chooses, mark his device or the labels or advertising matter to be attached thereto, with the statement either that " Patents are pending " or that " Patent is applied for." This has no effect to prevent infringement but is memely a warning to the public that they must keep off the ground, and that they are liable later to action for infringement if they do not. When the patent is granted, however, the law makes it obligatory upon the part of the inventor that he shall mark his invention patented, giving the date or number of the patent. If he does not do so he is liable to a fine of $100 for each offense. He will be unable to collect damages for the infringement of his patent for no notice has been given that the device is patented. The word " Patented " should be either formed upon the invention itself or printed upon labels or advertisements attached to the invention or in the case of a process printed in connection with any circulars or other matter relating to it.

While a patentee must mark his devices as patented, there is a heavy fine for those who use the word "Patented" on an unpatented appliance, for this tends to keep the public out of its rights.

CHAPTER IX.

Transfer of Patent Rights.

SELLING AND BUYING PATENTS AND RIGHTS THEREIN.

It is surprising how entirely careless inventors and vendors of patent rights are with regard to contracts, sales and other transfers.

In entering into a contract on any other subject, the services of an attorney are sought and the conditions of the contract are fully set forth. In buying land the deed will be scrutinized carefully, an abstract of title will be required, the title will be examined closely, and the deed finally, without fail, recorded. When a share in an invention is bought, however, or some right under a patent acquired, the parties seem to leave their wits and common sense at home. A mere verbal agreement is entered into, the rights are taken "unsight and unseen." Supposed transfers are made without expressed consideration or without any clear understanding between the parties as to the interest transferred. Contracts for manufacture and sale are entered into without only the vaguest statement of the duties and privileges of the respective parties.

And then the vendor or vendee wonder that trouble arises.

The same care should be taken in transferring either an interest in an invention or the Patent on it, that is taken in transferring an interest in any other piece of property. The vendor should see that provision is made for future payments or the reversion of the interest transferred, in case these payments are not made or the terms of the agreement carried out. The vendee should see that the vendor has something to be transferred, that the transfer is in proper legal form, definitely covering the subject-matter, and that the transfer is properly recorded.

There are Three Forms of Transfer:
Assignment. Grant. License.

An assignment is that form of deed which transfers either, 1st: *all the right* and title to an invention for *all the territory* and the *whole term* of the Patent, or 2d: which transfers an *undivided interest* in the Patent for all of the country and all of the term.

(1) By the first of these transfers all right, title and interest passes to the assignee and the assignor has no further interest in the invention, except in the case of his agreeing to receive his consideration in installments. Even then his interest is in getting his money,— not in the invention which he has completely parted with.

(2) By the second transfer, the assignee and assignor are made tenants in common. Each has as much right as the other to the invention, each is free to use, manufacture or sell or to license others to do so. Neither can, however, transfer a greater interest than he has. Thus an assignee of an undivided interest cannot assign the whole title. He can, however, make any transfer of a subordinate right or interest not greater than his own.

An assignment should be in writing signed by the assignor and under seal. It should expressly convey an interest in the invention itself and the patent therefor and not merely in one of the privileges under the Patent. A mere contract to sell an invention to a prospective buyer is not an assignment (*see* Contract of Sale).

.An assignment is of the invention itself and may be made either before an application is filed, before the Patent issues, or afterwards.

If made before filing, the assignment should refer to the date on which the application was executed and should be forwarded with the application papers.

If made after filing but before the issue of a Patent, the Serial Number and date of the application should be given.

If made after Patent has issued the Number and date of the Patent should be stated. (Each application for patent, or Patent should either have its own specific assignment or be specifically referred to in a blanket assignment.)

This is so that the Patent Office may identify the particular invention transferred. This identification is as necessary with patents as in a deed of land. To properly record the assignment the invention must be identified and the only means of doing this is by reference to an application. A transfer of an invention generally, will not cover all the patents which may be necessary to protect that invention. Each patent or application should be specifically referred to.

Recording. This is a matter in which the Vendee of a Patent should take especial care. In order to protect innocent third parties who, ignorant of a former transfer, purchase an interest in an invention, the law provides that all transfers shall be recorded in the United States Patent Office within three months of their execution.

If not recorded, the first transfer is not valid against innocent third parties, though it is still good as against the original transferer.

Immediately upon the assignment of a Patent send the document to " The Commissioner of Patents," Washington, D. C., together with a fee of $1.00 for three hundred words or under. For documents of over three hundred words and under a thousand words the recording fee is $2.00. For over a thousand words $3.00 is required.   Upon the receipt of the fee the document will be recorded and in time returned to the sender.

A grant is precisely like an assignment except that it transfers the entire or an undivided interest in a certain specified *territory less than the whole* of the United States.   A grant like an assignment conveys in its territory the *exclusive* right to make *and* sell *and* use.   In this it differs from a license, which operates on only one or two of these privileges, as to make or sell: To make and use, or to make and sell and use.

A grant, like an assignment, may be given with certain conditions as to the number of constructions to be used or put up, or as to the mode in which the invention may be used.   Unless expressly stated, the vendees of the grantee may *use* the invention in any part of the United States, though the grantee himself is restricted in making and selling to a certain territory.

License.   Any transfer of an interest less than the whole interest or an undivided portion of such whole interest operates as a license.

Transfers of the exclusive right to use, or the exclusive right to sell, or the exclusive right to make, or to make and sell, etc., etc., are licenses.

Transfers of the exclusive right to use for a particular purpose, or to make in a certain manner are licenses.   **L. OF C.**

Transfers of the exclusive right to make *and* use *and* sell in a *particular form* or for some *special purpose* are licenses.

In all of these cases the licensor retains some right as his own and the full and entire rights to the invention over the whole country or some specified part of it are not given.

A transfer of a right to make and sell is, however, an assignment or grant, because the right to use necessarily goes with the right to sell and is implied thereby, else would the buyer have no right to use what he had bought.

A license may be either exclusive or non-exclusive and may be either oral or written. A license does not have to be recorded. Two forms of license are subjoined.

Contracts for the Future Transfer of Rights to an Invention. These contracts mostly arise when an invention is not completed nor Patent applied for. The inventor transfers an interest in his invention and agrees to transfer an interest in his patents thereon.

This contract is not an assignment but only an agreement to assign. It conveys only an equitable interest which equitable right may be enforced in a Court of Equity by a suit to compel specific performance.

This problem often confronts the inventor and the prospective vendee. What means can be taken to protect the vendee from an inventor refusing to assign his Patents or the completed invention where the consideration has passed? And on the other hand, when the assignment or transfer is made first and the money paid in installments, how may the inventor protect himself.

The best way is by putting the assignment in escrow. That is, putting it in the hands of some third party to whom the money is to be paid, or who will turn over the assignment when the money is all paid. This is fair to both parties. The vendee is protected for the assignment is made. The inventor is protected for the assignment is not to be turned over until the consideration is all paid.

Expressing the conditions of the transfer or agreement. If there are conditions to be fulfilled by the transferee, as the payment of installments, the payment of royalties, the perfecting or exploiting of an invention, its advertising and pushing,— have these conditions clearly and distinctly stated. Give the dates on which the installments or royalties shall become due, the manner in which they shall be paid, the amount of advertising to be done, its character, or the way in which the invention shall be pushed, or the degree of excellence in construction to which the manufacturer shall be held.

If possible, have a clause inserted in the agreement requiring the Assignee, Grantee or Licensee to manufacture or sell at least a certain quantity or to pay royalties on a certain minimum quantity of the goods, whether he sells them or not. This compels him to exert himself and the invention cannot lie entirely unused on the shelf.

With a statement of any of the conditions above expressed there should be a clause calling for the abrogation of the contract or transfer and all rights conveyed thereby if anyone of the conditions is not fulfilled.

Many manufacturers refuse to make any minimum guarantee under any circumstances. The inventor's insistence thereon should depend on circumstances and the standing and reliability of the party he is dealing with. The lack of such a clause, however, often results in an invention being laid on the shelf, not put on sale, and not used, to the inventor's loss.

The transfer of foreign rights. A transfer of the rights to an invention or of rights in a United States Patent does not operate as a transfer of the foreign rights. Such transfer can only be made by a conveyance specifically referring to the foreign Patents, and properly recorded in the foreign country. An agreement to transfer foreign patent rights can, however, be enforced by a Court of Equity, compelling the promiser to execute the transfer.

The various rights of buyers and sellers of Patents, their interests and their relations to each other and to the public cannot be considered within the limits of this book and must form the subject of another volume wherein the whole subject of buying and selling patent rights will be treated.

Foreign patents. The costs, conditions, terms, and all other data as to Patents in foreign countries will be treated at length in another volume of this series.

Assignment.

Of an Entire Interest in an Invention before the Issue of Letters Patent

Whereas I,   of   , county of and State of   , have invented certain and new and useful improvements in for which I am about to make application for letters patent of the United States; and whereas   of   , county of   , and State of   , is desirous of acquiring an interest in said invention and in the letters patent to be obtained therefor:

Now, therefore, to all whom it may concern, be it known, that, for and in consideration of the sum of   dollars, to me in hand paid, the receipt of which is hereby acknowledged, I, the said   have sold, assigned, and transferred, and by these presents do sell, assign and transfer, unto the said   the full and exclusive right to the said invention, as fully set forth and described

in the specification prepared and executed by me
on the   day of   , 19 , preparatory
to obtaining letters patent of the United States
therefor; and I do hereby authorize and request
the Commissioner of Patents to issue the said letters patent to the said   as the assignee
of my entire right, title and interest in and to the
same, for the sole use and behoof of the said
          and his legal representatives.

In testimony whereof I have hereunto set my
hand and affixed my seal this   day of   ,

.

. . . .

In presence of —

. . . .

. . . .

Territorial Interest After Grant of Patent.

Whereas I,   , of   , county of
          , State of   , did obtain letters patent
of the United States for improvement in
which letters patent are numbered   , and
bear date the   day of   , in the year
19 ; and whereas I am now the sole owner of
the said patent and of all rights under the same
in the below-recited territory; and whereas
of   , county of   , State of

is desirous of acquiring an interest in the same:

Now, therefore, to all whom it may concern, be it known that, for and in consideration of the sum of   dollars to me in hand paid, the receipt of which is hereby acknowledged, I, the said   , have sold, assigned and transferred, and by these presents do sell, assign and .transfer unto the said   , all the right, title and interest in and to the said invention, as secured to me by said letters patent, for, to and in the State of   , and for, to, or in no other place or places; the same to be held and enjoyed by the said   , within, and throughout the above specified territory but not elsewhere, for his own use and behoof, and for the use and behoof of his legal representatives, to the full end of the term for which said letters patent are or may be granted, as fully and entirely as the same would have been held and enjoyed by me had this assignment and sale not been made.

In testimony whereof I have hereunto set my hand and affixed my seal at   , in the county of   , and State of   , this   day of   , 19 .

....

In presence of

License - - Shop Right.

In consideration of the sum of   dollars,
to be paid by the firm of   , of   ,
in the county of   , State of   , I do
hereby license and empower the said   to
manufacture in said   (or other place
agreed upon) the improvement in
for which letters patent of the United States No.
     ,   were granted to me the   day of
        , in the year 19 , and to sell the machines
so manufactured throughout the United States to
the full end of the term for which said letters
patent are granted.

Signed at   , in the county of   and
State of   , this   day of   , 19 .

. . . .

In presence of —

. . . .

. . . .

Agreement to Assign.

This agreement, made this   day of
19 , by and between John Doe, of
county of   , and State of   , party of the
first part; and Jacob Stiles of   , county of

, and State of   (or the John Jones Company, a corporation organized under the laws of the State of   , and doing business at   ) party of the second part, witnesseth:

That whereas John Doe has invented certain new and useful improvements in   on which he is about to take out Letters Patent and of which a drawing (blue-print, photograph or other memoranda) is attached; and whereas the said party of the second part is desirous of acquiring an interest in the same;

Now, therefore, be it agreed between the parties hereto that for and in consideration of the sum of one dollar in hand paid to the party of the first part, and other valuable considerations (here set forth conditions in detail, if desired) the said party of the first part hereby transfers to the party of the second part, the   (here set forth the interest transferred) of his entire right, title and interest in and to the said invention; and he hereby agrees that when the patent or patents on this said   (title of invention) are prepared that he will execute an assignment (grant, or license) to the said party of the second part.

And the party of the first part further agrees that he will give to the party of the second part an option on all future inventions relating to the subject matter of the invention herewith referred to and will submit said inventions to the party of the second part for his acceptance before presenting

them to others and will assign said inventions to
the party of the second part upon the receipt of
suitable consideration to be at that time determined.

In witness whereof the parties above named hereto set their hands and seals this   , day of   ,

. . . .

In presence of —

25c. BOOKS.

ELECTRICITY. The study of, and its laws for beginners, comprising the laws of electric current generation and flow, Ohm's law, galvanism, magnetism, induction, principles of dynamos and motors, wiring, with explanations of simple mathematics as applied to electrical calculations. By N. H. SCHNEIDER. With 55 original illustrations and 6 tables.

DRY BATTERIES. A practical handbook on the designing, filling and finishing of dry batteries, with tables, for automobiles, gas engine, medical and coil work, electric bells, alarms, telephones, experiments and all purposes requiring a first-rate battery. Fully illustrated with 30 original drawings.

ELECTRICAL CIRCUITS AND DIAGRAMS. Being a selection of original up-to-date and practical diagrams for installing annunciators, alarms, bells, electric gas lighting, telephones, electric power light and wiring circuits, induction coils, gas engine igniters, dynamos and motors, armature windings. By N. H. SCHNEIDER.

ELECTRIC BELLS AND ALARMS. How to install them. By N. H. SCHNEIDER. Including batteries, wire and wiring, circuits, pushes, bells, burglar alarms, high and low water alarms, fire alarms, thermostats, annunciators, and the locating and remedying of faults. With 56 original diagrams.

MODERN PRIMARY BATTERIES. Their construction, use and maintenance, including batteries for telephones, telegraphs, motors, electric lights, induction coils, and for all experimental work. By N. H. SCHNEIDER. 94 pages, 55 illustrations. The best and latest American book on the subject.

EXPERIMENTING WITH INDUCTION COILS. H. S. NORRIE, author of "Induction Coils and Coil Making." A most instructive little book, full of practical and interesting experiments, fully explained in plain language with numerous hints and suggestions for evening entertainments. Arranged under the following headings: Introduction; The Handling of Ruhmkorff Coil; Experiments with Sparks; Effects in the Vacuum; Induction and Wireless Telegraphy. With 36 original illustrations. [In the press]

SMALL ACCUMULATORS. How made and used, by P. MARSHALL. Giving full descriptions how to make all the parts. assemble them, charge the cells and run them, with examples of their practical application. Useful receipts and memoranda and a glossary of technical terms. 80 pages, 40 illustrations, paper.

ELECTRIC GAS LIGHTING. How to install Electric gas igniting apparatus including the jump spark and multiple systems for all purposes. Also the care and selection of suitable batteries, wiring and repairs, by H. S. NORRIE. 101 pages, 57 illustrations, paper

25 Cent Books.

INDUCTION COILS. How to Make and Use Them, by P. MARSHALL. New edition revised and enlarged by K. STOYE. A practical handbook on the construction and use of medical and sparking coils for automobiles and gas engines. Fully illustrated with table of windings for coils of ¼ inch to 12 inch sparks.

THE MAGNETO TELEPHONE. Its construction, fitting up and use, by NORMAN HUGHES. Giving full particulars for planning out a short line, putting up the insulators, stringing wires, connecting instruments, with suitable batteries. **80 pages, 23 illustrations, including a number of diagrams of circuits.**

PRACTICAL ELECTRICS. A universal handy book on everyday electrical matters, including connections, alarms, batteries, bells, carbons, induction and resistance coils, dynamos, measuring, microphones, motors, telephones, phonographs, photophones, etc. **135 pages, 126 illustrations.**

WIRELESS TELEGRAPHY. How to Make an Experimental Wireless Telegraph Outfit at Home, without much expense. By A. F. COLLINS. **Illustrated, with diagrams.**

ELECTRIC BELLS AND ALARMS. By F. E. POWELL. A handbook on their construction, installation and repair.

ELECTRIC BATTERIES. How to Make and Use Them. By P. MARSHALL. Dealing with a number of well-known types of batteries. Including the Grouping of Cells. **Illustrated.**

MODEL STEAM ENGINE DESIGN. A handbook for the Designer of small Model Steam Engines, including original tables and calculations for speed, power, proportions of pumps, compound engines, and valve diagrams. By ROBERT M. DE VIGNIER. Contents of Chapters: 1. Various Types. Speed of Model Engines. 2. Power Calculations. Materials. 3. Feed Pumps. 4. Compound Engines. 5. The Valve Diagram. 6. Engine Layout. Patterns. **102 pages, 34 illustrations.**

MODEL STEAM ENGINES. How to Understand Them and How to Run Them. By H. GREENLY. Including examples of stationary locomotive, portable and marine engines. With different kinds of boilers and methods of getting up steam, as well as engine details and valve mechanisms, etc. **87 pages and 55 illustrations.**

MODEL RAILWAYS. A handbook on the choice of Model Locomotives and Railway Equipment, including designs for rail formations, and Model Railway Signaling, by W. J. BASSETT-LOWKE. **72 pages, 76 illustrations.**

SIMPLE PHOTOGRAPHIC EXPERIMENTS. A series of instructive experiments in Practical Photography. By T. T. BAKER. **68 pages, 14 illustrations.**

25 Cent Books.

ELECTRIC LIGHTING for amateurs. The installation of electric light on a small scale, construction of lamps and lamp holders, switches, batteries and their connections. **With 45 illustrations**

SIMPLE ELECTRICAL WORKING MODELS. How to make them and how to use them. **With 43 illustrations.**

TELEPHONES AND MICROPHONES. Making and using simple forms of telephones and microphones. **With 29 illustrations.**

ELECTRICAL APPARATUS. Simply explained. An introductory handbook on the principles and working of some of the electrical appliances in general use. **80 pages, 35 illustrations.**

X-RAYS SIMPLY EXPLAINED. The theory and practical application of Radiography. **10 illustrations and 6 plates.**

STATIC ELECTRICITY. Simple experiments in. A series of instructive and entertaining electrical experiments with simple and inexpensive apparatus. **With 51 illustrations.**

SIMPLE SCIENTIFIC EXPERIMENTS. How to perform entertaining and instructive experiments with simple home-made apparatus. By A. DeRatti. **69 pages, 59 illustrations. 25c.**

COOLING TOWERS. Their prominence. Theory. History and development. The open type. The forced or fan draft type. The natural draft chimney type. Advantages of cooling tower. Economy and results in cooling; capacity and size. By Oswald Gueth, M.E. A very important work of considerable interest to engineers, and the designers of steam power plants. With numerous tables. **72 pages, 32 illustrations, paper. 25c.***

MECHANICAL REFRIGERATION SIMPLY EXPLAINED. Part I. Elementary treatise for operating Engineers. Cooling by means of expansion and evaporation. The ammonia compression system. Operation of the compressor. Refrigeration Plant. The Ammonia absorption system. Operation. Vogt absorption system. Isbel-Portor absorption system. Freezing Mixtures. Advantages of the absorption Machine. The Vacuum system. Capacity of Ice-Making Machines. Can and plate systems compared. Tables, etc., etc. **71 pages, 18 illustrations, paper, 25c.**

PUMP MANUAL FOR ENGINEERS. A practical treatise on different kinds of pumps for engineers, including a chapter on Designing Pumps, by R. H. Brooks. Pumping machinery for Acid Water by Kresse. Hydrant and Hose Pipe Data, Installation of Pumps in Power Plants. **With numerous tables, illustrations, notes and useful information.**

SMALL ELECTRICAL MEASURING INSTRUMENTS. How to make and use them. A practical handbook describing the making and using of Measuring Instruments. Contents of Chapters: 1. Galvanometers for Testing the Presence of an Electric Current. 2. Voltmeters, for Measuring the Pressure or Quantity of an Electric Current. 3. Wheatstone Bridge, for Measuring Electrical Resistance. 4. Instruments for Measuring Static Electricity. 5. Practical Details of Construction. 6. The Principles upon which Electrical Measuring Instruments Work. 7. How to Use the Instruments. 8. How to Choose them. **90 pages 59 illustrations.**

SMALL ELECTRIC MOTORS HOW TO MAKE AND USE THEM. By F. E. POWELL. Contents of Chapters: Preface. 1. Some Points in the Design of Electromotors. 2. Examples of Small Motors to be Worked by Battery Power. 3. A Model Four-pole Electromotor. 4. Motors for Use on Electric Lighting Circuits. 5. Applications of Small Motors and the Power Required for Certain Work. 6. Starting and Speed Controlling Switches; Fuses. 7. Reversing Switches for Model Motors; Gearing; tables for Windings. **75 pages, 48 detail drawings.**

SMALL DYNAMOS AND MOTORS. How to make and use them. A practical handbook, by F. E. POWELL. Contents of Chapters: 1. General Considerations. 2. Field Magnets. 3. Armatures. 4. Commutators and Other Details. 5. Tables of Windings. 6. How to Build a Small Machine. 7. Useful Data. 8. Testing and Repairing. **76 pages fully illustrated with detail drawings.**

SIMPLE CHEMICAL EXPERIMENTS. A series of instructive experiments in inorganic chemistry. By T. T. BAKER, S.C.S. The subject is treated in a simple manner in plain language, yet the experiments given will afford hours of amusement and instruction. **72 pages, 19 illustrations. 25c.**

DESIGN SHEETS. Direct current dynamos. These sheets are for carrying out dynamo designs according to the method laid down by S. P. THOMPSON. 1. General Description of the Machine and the Commercial Test. 2 and 3. Schedule for Electrical, Mechanical and Magnetic Test. 4. Schedule for the Calculation of Armature Winding and Field. 5. Temperature Test; and Estimate of Weights and Costs. Five sheets, 8 x 10½ in. **Price per set, 25c.** Special price on a quantity. Each sheet has two holes punched in one end for easy filing. Printed on good ledger paper.

MAGNETISM CURVES OF MAGNETIC DATA for various materials, viz:—Sankey's " Lohys " Sheet Iron; Hadfield's Magnet Steel; Edgar Allen's Cast Steel; Krupp's Dynamo-magnet Steel; Wrought Iron (Hopkinson); Grey Cast Iron (Hopkinson); Cast Iron (Parshall); Sheet Steel (acid open-hearth process (H. S. Meyer); Styrian Iron Sheet (Blathy); and Curve for Air, the abscissæ being in ampere-turns per one-hundredth of an inch of magnetic path. A reprint on transparent paper for office use of Plate I. of Thompson's Dynamo-Electric Machinery, Vol. I., measuring 25 in. by 16 in. **25 cts.**

WIRELESS TELEGRAPHY FOR AMATEURS. A handbook on the Principles of Radiotelegraphy and the construction and working of apparatus for short Distance Transmission. By R. P. Howgrave-Graham. This is a most important new work for the amateur who wishes to make apparatus that are not mere toys. While the author gives all the technical information that is necessary, the best part of the book is devoted to practical details, construction and operation, making the book one of the most valuable on this subject. Contents of Chapters: Preface. 1. History and Principles of Radio-Telegraphy. 2. The Poulsen System of Generating Electric Waves for Radiotelegraphy. 3. Practical Radiotelegraphy, Transmitting Apparatus. 4. Receiving Apparatus. Appendix. **160 pages, 51 illustrations, 12mo., cloth. $1.00.‡**

THE A B C OF THE TELEPHONE By J. E. Homans. While this work is strictly elementary in the sense that it begins with the elements it nevertheless gives a very comprehensive survey of the entire field of telephone apparatus and construction including an excellent chapter on the theory of sound and another on the fundamental principles of electricity. Written in plain language it is a book that can be recommended. The work is divided into 29 chapters and contains 375 pages, 268 illustrations and diagrams, 12mo., cloth. **$1.00.***

PRIVATE HOUSE ELECTRIC LIGHTING. A popular handbook on modern methods in wiring and fitting as applied to private houses, including a chapter on small generating plants. By F. H. Taylor. 2d edition, rewritten. Contents of Chapters: 1. Systems of Supply. 2. Systems of Wiring. 3. Arrangements of Circuits and Conductors, etc. 4. Arrangements of Lights and Switches. 5. The Testing of an Installation. 6. The Materials and Accessories used. 7. Cost of Installation Work. 8. Cost of Using Electric Light. 9. Generating Plant. **132 pages, 66 illustrations, 12mo., boards. 50c.***

GROUPING OF ELECTRIC CELLS. A treatise on. By F. W. Hunton. Treating of the numerous forms and grouping of electric cells for convenience, economy, efficiency and other reasons. Part I.—The Grouping of Similar Cells for Greatest Current. Introductory. Regular Groups. Irregular Points and General Rule. Part II.—The Economical of Similar Cells. The Shortest Group. The Smallest Group. Index, with numerous formulas. * pages, 16mo., cloth. **60c.‡**

PRACTICAL ELECTRICS. A universal handbook on everyday electrical matters, electric burglar and other alarms, different kinds of primary and secondary batteries, electric bells and annunciator system, carbons, connections, induction coils, resistance and intensity coils, dynamo-electric machines, magneto dynamos, construction, fire-risks, wires, lamps, measuring instruments, construction of microphones, phonographs; and photophones; motors; storage batteries; telephones; circuits and calls, etc., **135 pages, 96 illustrations, 8vo., cloth. 75c.**

25c. BOOKS.

MODEL BOILER MAKING. Contains full instructions for ⌐signing and making model stationary, marine and locomot⌐ boilers. Fully illustrated with original working drawings.

METAL WORKING TOOLS AND THEIR USES. A Handb⌐ for Young Engineers and Apprentices. Shows how to use sim⌐ tools required in metal working and model making. Illustrated.

SIMPLE MECHANICAL WORKING MODELS. How to ma⌐ and use them, including stationary engine locomotive, steambo⌐ waterwheel, etc. With 34 illustrations.

MODEL STEAMER BUILDING. A practical handbook on ⌐ design and construction of model steamer hulls, and fittings, w⌐ 39 scale drawings.

MACHINERY FOR MODEL STEAMERS. On the design, c⌐ struction, fitting and erecting of engines and boilers for model stea⌐ ers, with 44 scale drawings.

THE SLIDE VALVE. Simply explained for working eng⌐ eers. Fully illustrated.

THE LOCOMOTIVE, simply explained. A first introduction⌐ the study of the locomotive engine, their designs, construction ⌐ erection, with a short catechism, and 26 illustrations.

THE BEGINNER'S GUIDE TO THE LATHE. An element⌐ instruction book on turning in wood and metal. By P. Marsha⌐ 76 pages, 75 illustrations.

GAS AND OIL ENGINES. A practical handbook on, with⌐ structions for care and running. Illustrated.

STANDARD SCREW THREADS. A Guide to Standard Scr⌐ Threads and Twist Drills. (Small sizes.) Illustrated.

STEAM TURBINES. How to design and build them. A pr⌐ tical handbook for model makers. Contents of Chapters. 1. Gene⌐ Consideration. 2, Pressure Developed by an Impinging Jet; Veloc⌐ and Flow of Steam Through Orifices. 3. Method of Designing⌐ Steam Turbine. 4. Complete Designs f⌐r DeLaval Steam Turbin⌐ Method of Making Vanes; Shrouding. 5. The Theory of Multi⌐ Stage Turbines. Fully illustrated with detail drawings and tables⌐

MECHANICAL DRAWING, simply explained. Use of inst⌐ ments, reading and setting out drawings, inking in and finishi⌐ drawings for reproduction, lettering, with 44 illustrations.

ACETYLENE GAS. How to make and use it. A practi⌐ handbook on the uses of Acetylene Gas, suitable apparatus for⌐ generation, hints and fitting up, etc. 34 illustrations.

50 Cent Books.

PRACTICAL DYNAMO AND MOTOR CONSTRUCTION. A Handbook of Constructive Details and Workshop Methods used in Building Small Machines. By ALFRED W. MARSHALL. Contents Chapters: 1. Field Magnets. 2. Winding Field Magnets. 3. Drum Armature Building. 4. Ring Armature Building. 5. How to Wind Armatures. General Notes. Siemens or H Armatures. Star Armatures. 6. How to Wind Armatures (continued). Drum and Ring Armatures. Binding Wires and Repairs. 7. Commutator Making. 8. Brush Gears. 9. Mechanical Details of Dynamos and Motors. 10. Terminals and Connections. **131 pages, 133 illustrations, 12mo., boards. 50c.***

SMALL ACCUMULATORS. How made and used. An elementary Handbook for the use of amateurs and students. By PERCIVAL MARSHALL, A.I.M.E. Contents of Chapters: 1. The Theory of the Accumulator. 2. How to Make a 4-Volt Pocket Accumulator. 3. How to Make a 32-Ampere Hour Accumulator. 4. Types of Small Accumulators. 5. How to Charge and Use Accumulators. Applications of Small Accumulators, Electrical Novelties, etc. Glossary of Technical Terms. **80 pages. 40 illustrations. 12mo., cloth. 50c.**

THE MAGNETO-TELEPHONE. Its construction, fitting up and adaptability to everyday use. By NORMAN HUGHES. Contents of Chapters: Some Electrical Considerations: 1. Introductory. 2. Construction. 3. Lines, Indoor Lines. 4. Signaling Apparatus. 5. Batteries. Open Circuit Batteries. Closed Circuit Batteries. Practical Operations. Circuit with Magneto Bells and Lightning Testers. How to Test the Line. Push-Button Magneto Circuit. Two Stations with Battery Bells. 7. Battery Telephone. Battery Telephone Circuit. Three Instruments on one Line. 8. General Remarks. Index. **80 pages, 23 illustrations, 12mo., cloth. 50c.**

ELECTRIC GAS LIGHTING. How to install electric gas igniting apparatus, including the jump spark and multiple system for use in houses, churches, theatres, halls, schools, stores or any large building. Also the care and selection of suitable Batteries, Wiring and Repairs. By H. S. NORRIE (author of Induction Coils and Coil Making). Contents of Chapters: 1. Introduction. Means of Producing Sparks, Induction, Induction Coils. 2. Application of Induction Coils to Gas Lighting. Forms of Burners used, Pendant, Rachet, Arm, Welsbach, Automatic Burners for Gasolene and Acetylene. How to Connect up Apparatus. Wiring a House. Locating Leaks or Short Circuits. Wiring in finished Houses. General Remarks. 4. Primary Coils and Safe Devices. 5. How to Wire and Fit up Different Systems for Lightning Large Buildings. 6. The Selection of Suitable Batteries for Gas Lighting, Repairs, Maintenance, etc. **108 pages, 57 illustrations and diagrams, cloth. 50c.**

JUST OUT.

293 pages, 298 illustrations, 8vo.
Cloth, $1.00 net.

===THE===

MODEL LIBRARY

VOL. I.

Consisting of the following four American books,
with very complete general index.

The Study of Electricity and Its Laws
for Beginners.

How to Install Electric Bells, Annunciators and Alarms.

Dry Batteries, How to Make and Use
Them.

Electrical Circuits and Diagrams. Illus
trated and explained.

THE PRACTICAL ENGINEER'S HANDBOOK.

TO THE CARE AND MANAGEMENT OF

ELECTRIC POWER PLANTS

By NORMAN H. SCHNEIDER,

Chief Engineer, "White City," Colingwood, Ohio.

EXTRACTS FROM PREFACE.

In revising the first edition of Power Plants the author decided greatly enlarge it in the hope that it will have a still greater ccess than the first one. The section on theory is thoroughly vised. A complete chapter on Standard Wiring including new bles and original diagrams added. The National Fire Under-iters' rules condensed and simple explanations given. Direct and alternating current motors have been given a special apter and modern forms of starting rheostats described at length. Ie principles of alternators have been considered also trans-rmers and their applications. Modern testing instruments and eir use are given a separate chapter. New matter has been ded to storage batteries including charging of automobile bat-ries, 10 new tables, and 137 new illustrations.

SYNOPSIS OF CONTENTS OF CHAPTERS.

1. THE ELECTRIC CURRENT; series and multiple connections; sistance of circuits; general explanation of formulas.
2. STANDARD WIRING; wiring formulas and tables; wiring sys-ns; cut-outs; conduits; panel boxes; correct methods of wiring.
3. DIRECT AND ALTERNATING CURRENT GENERATORS; manage-nt in the power house; windings; selection of generators.
4. MOTORS AND MOTOR STARTERS; various forms of motors; con-llers; care of motors and their diseases; rules for installing.
5. TESTING AND MEASURING INSTRUMENTS; voltmeter testing d connections; instruments used; switchboard instruments.
6. THE STORAGE BATTERY; different kinds; switchboards for arging fixed and movable batteries; management of battery.
7. THE INCANDESCENT LAMP; various methods of testing; life lamps.
8. ENGINEERING NOTES; belts and pulleys h.p. of belts. Tables. ntents. Index.

290 pages, 203 illustrations. 12mo., cloth, $1.50.
Full limp leather, $2.50.

A MANUAL ON

THE CARE AND HANDLING

OF

ELECTRIC PLANTS.

Written for the practical engineer and adapted to the United Sta
military Service. Including Dynamos, Motors, Wiring, Storag
Batteries, Testing Instruments, Incandescent Lamps, Photometry and a chapter on the Oil Engine.

By NORMAN H. SCHNEIDER.

Late Electrical Expert, Southern Artillery District, New York.

Author of "Induction Coils and Coil Making," " Notes on Uni
States Army Power Plants," etc.

This manual is intended as a practical handbook for electricia
engineers' assistants and all who are interested in the operation
commercial or military electric plants. The basis of the work w
a number of notes and memoranda accumulated by the autl
during ten years of practical work and upon several courses
lectures delivered at Fort Wadsworth to officers of the U. S. Ar
lery, and also to non-commissioned officers." The chapter
incandescent lamps is especially valuable as this is a subject vi
little touched upon in other works. The selection of tables will
found very useful for reference. *Contents of Chapters:* 1. 1
Electric Current, Insulators, Conductors, Series and Multi
Connections, Wiring, etc.; 2. Dynamos and Motors, Varieties
Motors, Management, Equalizers, Starting boxes, Sparking a
Heating Brushes, Practical Hints, etc.; 3. Electrical Measur
Instruments and how to use them; 4. The Storage Battery and
management, Testing, Equipments, Fluids, various Switchboa
and their working, etc.; 5. The Incandescent Lamp, Testing, Lif
Lamps, Photometry, etc.; 6. The Oil Engine, Belting, Lining
Engine, Pulleys, etc.; Index. 113 pages, illustrated with
original drawings and numerous useful tables.

Bound in limp leather, pocket size. By mail for $1.

ELECTRICAL INSTRUMENTS AND TESTING

How to Use the Voltmeter, Ammeter, Galvanometer, Potentiometer, Ohmmeter, the Wheatstone Bridge, and the Standard Portable Testing Sets.

BY NORMAN H. SCHNEIDER.

THIRD EDITION WITH NEW CHAPTERS ON

TESTING WIRES AND CABLES AND LOCATING FAULTS

In Telegraph and Telephone Systems.

BY JESSE HARGRAVE,

Assistant Electrical Engineer, Postal Telegraph Cable Co.

The fact that two editions of this book have already been sold proves the utility of this work. The publishers, however, determined to make it still more complete and up to date by adding additional chapters especially for telephone and telegraph wire men. The new information was prepared by an authority.

The first chapters of the work describe the various forms of electrical testing and measuring instruments and their construction.

The balance of the work is devoted to practical measuring and testing, using the different instruments described and including tests for insulation, resistance, current and e.m.f. made with a voltmeter, as well as many telephone and telegraph tests.

In working out the many practical examples simple algebraic formulas only are used and these are fully explained in plain language. Most of the diagrams have been specially drawn for this book. The work is divided into XIII chapters as follows:

Introduction. Chapters I and II, The Galvanometer. III, Rheostats. IV, The Voltmeter. V, The Wheatstone Bridge. VI, Forms of Portable Sets. VII, Current Flow and e.m.f. VIII, The Potentiometer. IX, Condensers, X, Cable Testing. XI, Testing with Voltmeter. XII, Testing Telegraph Wires and Cables. XIII, Locating Faults in Telegraph and Telephone Wires and Cables. Tables. Index.

256 pages, 133 illustrations and diagrams, 12mo., cloth, $1.00‡ Full limp leather, $2.00.‡

AN AMERICAN BOOK.

INDUCTION COILS and COIL MAKING.

Second edition thoroughly revised, greatly enlarged and brought up to latest American Practice,

BY H. S. NORRIE,
(NORMAN H. SCHNEIDER)

Considerable space in the new matter is given to the following Medical and bath coils, gas engine and spark coils, contact breakers primary and secondary batteries; electric gas lighting; new method of X-ray work, etc. A complete chapter on up-to-date wireless telegraphy; a number of new tables and 25 original illustrations. Great care has been given to the revision to make this book the best American work on the subject. A very complete index, contents, list of illustrations and contents of tables have been added.

Contents of Chapters.

1. Construction of coils; sizes of wire; winding; testing; insulation; general remarks; medical and spark coils. 2. Contact breakers 3. Insulation and cements. 4. Construction of condensers. 5. Experiments. 6. Spectrum analysis. 7. Currents in vacuo; air pumps 8. Rotating effects. 9. Electric gas lighting; in multiple; in series 10. Primary batteries for coils; varieties; open circuit cells; closed circuit cells; solutions. 11. Storage or secondary batteries; construction; setting up; charging. 12. Tesla and Hertz effects. 13. Roentgen Radiography. 14. Wireless telegraphy; arrangement of circuit of coil and coherer for sending and receiving messages; coherers; translating devices; air conductors; tables; contents; index.

XII + 270 Pages, 79 Illustrations, 5 x 6½ Inches. Cloth, $1.00.

Design of Dynamos

BY

SILVANUS P. THOMPSON, D. Sc., B. A., F. R. S.

EXTRACTS FROM PREFACE.

" The present work is purposely confined to continuous current generators. The calculations and data being expressed in inch measures; but the author has adopted throughout the decimal subdivision of the inch; small lengths being in mils, and small areas of cross-section in sq. mils, or, sometimes, also, in circular mils."

CONTENTS OF CHAPTERS.

1. Dynamo Design as an Art.

2. Magnetic Data and Calculations. Causes of waste of Power. Coefficients of Dispersion. Calculation of Dispersion. Determination of exciting ampere-turns. Example of Calculation.

3. Copper Calculations. Weight of Copper Wire. Electrical resistance of Copper, in cube, strip, rods, etc. Space-factors. Coil Windings; Ends; Insulation; Ventilating; Heating.

4. Insulating Materials and Their Properties. A list of materials, including " Armalac," " Vitrite," " Petrifite," " Micanite," " Vulcabeston," " Stabilite," " Megohmite," etc. With tables.

5. Armature Winding Schemes. Lap Windings, Ring Windings, Wave Windings, Series Ring-Windings, Winding Formulæ. Number of circuits. Equalizing connections. Colored plates.

6. Estimation of Losses, Heating and Pressure-drop. Copper Losses, Iron Losses, Excitation Losses, Commutator Losses, Losses through sparking. Friction and Windage Losses. Secondary Copper Losses.

7. The Design of Continuous Current Dynamos. Working Constants and Trial Values; Flux-densities; Length of Air-gap; Number of Poles; Current Densities; Number of Armature Conductors; Number of Commutator Segments; Size of Armature (Steinmetz coefficient); Assignment of Losses of Energy; Centrifugal Forces; Calculation of Binding Wires; Other procedure in design. Criteria of a good design. Specific utilization of material.

8. Examples of Dynamo Design.
1. Shunt-wound multipolar machine, with slotted drum armature. 2. Over-compounded Multipolar traction generator, with slotted drum armature, with general specifications, tables, dimensions and drawings, fully described.

A number of examples of generators are given in each chapter, fully worked out with rules, tables and data,

VIII.×253 pages, 92 illustrations, 10 large folding plates and 4 Three-color Plates, 8vo., cloth, $3.50.

ALGEBRA SELF-TAUGHT.

BY

W. PAGET HIGGS, M.A., D.Sc.

FOURTH EDITION.

CONTENTS.

Symbols and the signs of operation. The equation and the un-known quantity. Positive and negative quantities. Multiplication, involution, exponents, negative exponents, roots, and the use of ex-ponents as logarithms. Logarithms. Tables of logarithms and proportional parts. Transportation of systems of logarithms. Com-mon uses of common logarithms. Compound multiplication and the binomial theorem. Division, fractions and ratio. Rules for division. Rules for fractions. Continued proportion, the series and the sum-mation of the series. Examples. Geometrical means. Limit of series. Equations. Appendix. Index. 104 pages, 12mo, cloth, **60c.**

See also **Algebraic Signs**, Spons' Dictionary of Engineering No. 2. 40 cts.

See also **Calculus**, Supplement to Spons' Dictionary No. 5. 75 cts.

Barlow's Tables of squares, cubes, square roots, cube roots, reciprocals of all numbers up to 10,000. A thoroughly reliable work of 200 pages, 12mo, cloth, $2.50.

Logarithms.—Tables of logarithms of the natural numbers from 1 to 108,000 with constants. By CHARLES BABBAGE, M.A. 220 pages, 8vo, cloth, $3.00.

Logarithms.—A. B. C. Five figure logarithms for general use. By C. J. WOODWARD, B.Sc. 143 pages, complete thumb index. 12mo, limp leather, $1.60.

Books mailed post-paid to any address on receipt of price

Books for Steam Engineers.

DIGRAM OF CORLISS ENGINE. A large engraving giving a longitudinal section of the Corliss engine cylinder, showing relative positions of the piston, steam valves, exhaust valves, and wrist plates when cut-off takes place at $\frac{1}{4}$ stroke for each 15 degrees of the circle. With full particulars. Reach-rods and rock shafts. The circle explained. Wrist-plates and eccentrics. Explanation of figures, etc. Printed on heavy paper, size 13 in. x 19 in., **25c.**

THE CORLISS ENGINE and its Management. A Practical Handbook for young engineers and firemen, (3rd edition) by J. T. HENTHORN. A good little book, containing much useful and practical information. **Illustrated, cloth, $1.00.**

THE FIREMAN'S GUIDE to the Care and Management of Boilers, by KARL P. DAHLSTROM, M.E., covering the following subjects: Firing and Economy of Fuel; Feed and Water Line: Low Water and Priming: Steam Pressure: Cleaning and Blowing Out; General Directions. A thoroughly practical book. **Cloth, 50c.**

A B C OF THE STEAM ENGINE. With a description of the automatic shaft governor, with six large scale drawings. A practical handbook for firemen helpers and young engineers, giving a set of detail drawings all numbered and lettered and with names and particulars of all parts of an up-to-date American high speed stationary steam engine. Also a large drawing and full description of the automatic shaft governor. With notes and practical hints. This work will prove of great help to all young men who wish to obtain their engineer's license. **Cloth, price 50c.**

HOW TO RUN ENGINES AND BOILERS. By E. P. WATSON, (for many years a practical engineer, and a well-known writer in *The Engineer*.) A first-rate book for beginners, firemen and helpers. Commencing from the beginning, showing how to thoroughly overhaul a plant, foundations, lining up machinery, setting valves, vacuum, eccentrics, connection, bearings, fittings, cleaning boilers, water tube boilers, running a plant, and many useful rules, hints and other practical information; many thousands already sold. **160 pages, fully illustrated, cloth, $1.00.**

AMMONIA REFRIGERATION. By I. I. REDWOOD. A practical work of reference for engineers and others employed in the management of ice and refrigerating machinery. A first-rate book, beginning from the bottom and going carefully through the various processes, stage by stage, with many tables and original illustrations. **Cloth, $1.00.**

MEYER SLIDE VALVE. Position diagram of cylinder with cutoff at $\frac{1}{8}$, $\frac{1}{4}$, $\frac{3}{8}$ and $\frac{1}{2}$ stroke of piston with movable valves, on card 7$\frac{1}{2}$in. x 5$\frac{1}{2}$ in. **Price, 25c.**

Movable Valve Models, Diagrams and Charts.

MEYER'S VALVE. A position diagram of cylinder with cut-off at ⅛, ¼, ⅜ and ½ stroke of piston. By W. H. WEIGHTMAN. With movable valves. Printed on card. **25c. net.**

WORKING VALVE MODELS FOR MARINE ENGINEERS. A set of four cards: 1, Piston Valve with Steam Inside. 2, Piston Valve with Steam Outside. 3, Double-ported Slide Valve. 4, Common Slide Valve. Each card is in colors and has movable ports. Also full descriptive matter. In cloth case. **75c. net.**

WORKING MODELS OF ENGINE SLIDE VALVES. Comprising a complete set of eight diagrams in colors, with movable ports: 1, Short D Slide Valve. 2, Single-acting Piston Valve (for Steam Hammer). 3, Meyer's Variable Cut-off Valves. 4, Long D Slide Valve. 5, Short D Slide Valve (Balanced). 6, Marine Engine Piston Valve. 7, Double-ported Slide Valve. 8, Simple Trick Valve. With small booklet giving full instructions **$1.25 net.**

WORKING MODEL " X " SERIES NO. 1 and 2. No. 1 complete simple steam engine single cylinder horizontal type fitted with a D slide valve, sectional view showing all movable and fixed parts, drawn to scale, printed in colors on heavy card, size 6x9½ in. **$1.00 net, with book, $1.25 net.**

No. 2, complete single cylinder steam engine, horizontal girder type fitted with Meyer's valve gear, sectional view showing all movable and fixed parts drawn to scale, printed in colors on heavy card, size 6x9½ in. **$1.00 net, with book, $1.25 net.**

No. 1 and No. 2 together with book, $2.00 net. These are two exceptionally fine models, all moving parts so connected that there is practically no back lash, the relative positions of all moving parts are shown at every point in the stroke of the engine.

CORLISS ENGINE CHART. A fine engraving showing relative positions of the Piston Steam Valves, exhaust valves and wrist plates, etc., when cut-off takes place at ¼ stroke for each 15 degrees of circle, with full particulars. Size 13x19 in. **25c. Special price on a quantity.**

SLIDE VALVE CHART, showing position of the crank pin, eccentric, and piston at the point of admission, lead, full speed port opening, cut-off, release, full exhaust port opening and compression. With full directions. A blue print, 14¾x10¾.

LOCOMOTIVE CHARTS. American type, a transparent educational chart, with every part of the engine shown and numbered a good clear engraving size. 30x12 in. **25c.**

Atlantic type, a companion chart to above. **25c.**

THE COMPOUND ENGINE.

BY

W. J. TENNANT, A. M. I. Mech. E.

Author of " The Slide Valve Simply Explained."

―――――

" The author has treated his subject in a thorough, practical manner, yet in plain language, avoiding all mathematics. The numerous diagrams, scale drawings and illustrations add very considerably to its value. It is a work that should be in the hands of every progressive young steam engineer".

Contents of Chapters.

1. A General explanation of the Objects and Methods of Compounding.

2. The Transfer of Steam from the High-Pressure to the Low-Pressure Cylinder; The Intermediate Receiver.

3. The Size of the Low-Pressure Cylinder.

4. Back-Pressure in the High-Pressure Cylinder becomes Forward Pressure in the Low-Pressure Cylinder.

5. The near Equivalent of an Experimental Compound Engine, and of Steam for Working it; Guage-Pressure and Absolute-Pressure; Expansion-Diagram and Indicator Diagram.

6. Further Development of the Equivalent of a Sectional Compound Engine; its Mechanism.

7. Determination of " Drop " in the Receiver, and of the Pressure resulting when volumes of Steam at Different Pressures are put into communication with each other.

8. Final development of the near Equivalent of an Experimental Compound Engine.

9. Horse Power from Indicator-Diagram.

10. Reasons why the Compound Engine is Economical; The Heat Trap Theory; Cylinder Ratios and Receiver Proportions.

11. Receiver Proportions (*continued*).

12. Addition of Theoretical Curve of Expansion to Indicator Diagram; Superheat due to Drop.

13. Compounds, Triples and Quadruples; Steam Jackets.

14. The Condenser and Air Pump.

15. The Condenser and Air Pump, (*continued*).

Appendix; With tables of dimensions of various types of Compound Engines. **102 pages. With 63 illustrations, detail drawings and folding plates, 12mo., cloth, $1.00.‡**

Mechanical Draft.

BY

J. H. KINEALY, M. Am. Soc. M.E.

Past President American Society Heating and Ventilating Engineers.

PREFACE.

In writing this book the author has assumed that those who will use it are familiar with boilers and engine plants, and he has had in mind the practicing engineer who is called upon to design power plants, and who must therefore decide when it is best to use some form of mechanical draft. The arrangement of the book is what the experience of the author in making calculations for mechanical draft installations has shown him is probably the best. And he has tried to arrange the tables in such a way and in such a sequence that they may prove as useful to others as they have to him.

CONTENTS OF CHAPTERS.

1. GENERAL DISCUSSION. Introduction; systems of mechanical draft; chimneys v. mechanical draft; mechanical draft and economizers.

2. FORCED DRAFT. Systems; closed fire-room system; closed ashpit system; small fan required; usual pressure; forced draft and economisers; advantages; disadvantages.

3. INDUCED DRAFT. Introduction; temperature of gases; advantages; disadvantages.

4. FUEL AND AIR. Weight of coal to be burned; evaporation per lb. of coal; effect of rate of evaporation; weight of air required; volume of air and gases; volume of gases to handle; leakage; factor of safety.

5. DRAFT. Relation to rate of combustion; resistance of grate; resistance due to economizer; draft required under different conditions.

6. ECONOMIZERS. Effect of adding; ordinary proportion and cost; increase of temperature of feed water.

7. FANS. Type and proportions of fan used; relation between revolution of fan and draft; capacity of fan.

8. PROPORTIONING THE PARTS. Diameter of fan wheel required; speed at which the fan must run; power required to run the fan; size of engine required; steam used by fan engine; choosing the fan for forced draft, for induced draft without economizer, for induced draft with economizer; location of the fan; breeching and up-take; inlet chamber; discharge chimney; by-pass; water for bearings.

Appendix. Tables. Index. 156 pages. 13 plates. 16mo.

Cloth, $2.00.

MODEL RAILWAYS. A handbook on the choice of model locomotives and railway equipment, including designs for rail formations, and model railway signaling. By W. J. Bassett-Lowke. **72 pages, 80 illustrations, 8vo., paper. 25c.**

THE MODEL LOCOMOTIVE, its Design and Construction. A practical manual on the building and management of Miniature Railway Engines, by Henry Greenley. The book deals primarily with *working* model locomotives in all sizes, and for the most part for those built for the instruction and amusement of their owners. The subject is treated thoroughly and practically and profusely illustrated with details, diagrams and a number of large folding scale drawings. **276 pages, 9 in. x 5½ in., cloth. $2.50.‡**

THE WORLD'S LOCOMOTIVES. A digest of the latest locomotive practice in the railway countries of the world. By Chas. S. Lake. Contents of Chapters: 1. Introduction: Exigencies of Locomotive Design, Boiler Design and Construction. 2. Locomotive Types; Cylinder and Wheel Arrangements. 3. British Locomotives: 4-4-0 Type Express Engines. 4. British Locomotives: 4-4-2 Type Express Engines. 5. British Locomotives: Six Coupled, Single, and other Types of Express Engines. 6. British Locomotives: Tank Engines. 7. British Locomotives: Shunting, Contractors, Light Railway, and Crane Locomotives. 8. British Locomotives: Goods Engines. 9. British Compound Locomotives. 10 Colonial and Indian Locomotives. 11. Foreign Locomotives: Four-Coupled Express Engines. 12. Foreign Locomotives: 4-6-0 and other Types. 13. Foreign Locomotives: Tank Engines. 14. Foreign Locomotives: Goods Engines. 15. American Passenger Locomotives. 16. American Freight Locomotives. **380 pages, 376 illustrations, 8 large folding scale plates. 4to., cloth. $4.00 net.§**

MODERN BRITISH LOCOMOTIVES. By A. T. Taylor. 100 diagrams to scale, principal dimensions and tables. Preface. In compiling this volume, the author's object has been to produce a book of reference which he hopes may fill a gap which exists in the ranks of locomotive publications. No pains have been spared in making the information given as trustworthy as possible, and the author takes this opportunity of thanking the different locomotive engineers who have so courteously supplied the required information. The collection of diagrams represent the latest practice on all the leading railways of Great Britain. **118 pages, oblong, 8vo., cloth. $2.00.**

LOCOMOTIVE CATECHISM. Containing 1600 questions and answers. This book commends itself to every engineer and fireman who are anxious for promotion. Written in plain language. **450 pages, 223 illustrations, 24 folding plates, cloth. $2.00.‡**

LOCOMOTIVE SLIDE VALVE SETTING. A practical little treatise for the apprentice and all interested in locomotives. By C. E. Tulley. **31 pages, 29 illustrations, 16mo., limp cloth. 50c.**

Screw Cutting, Turning, Etc.

SCREW CUTTING. Turners' and fitters' pocket-book for calculating the change wheels for screws on a turning lathe and for a wheel cutting machine. By J. LA NICA. **16mo., paper. 20c.**

SCREW CUTTING. Turner's Handbook on Screw Cutting, Coning, etc., with tables, examples, gauges, and formulas. By WALTER PRICE. **8vo., cloth. 40c.**

SCREW CUTTING. Tables for engineers and mechanics, giving the values of the different trains of wheels required to produce screws of any pitch. By Lord Lindsay. **8vo., oblong. 80c.**

SCREW CUTTING. Screw cutting tables, for the use of Mechanical engineers, showing the proper arrangement of wheels for cutting the threads of screws of any required pitch, with a table for making the universal gas-pipe threads and taps. By W. A. MARTIN. Sixth edition. **Oblong, cloth. 40c.**

TURNING. The practice of hand-turning in wood, ivory, shell, etc., with instructions for turning such work in metal as may be required in the practice of turning in wood, ivory, etc., also an appendix on ornamental turning. (A book for beginners.) By FRANCIS CAMPIN. Third edition. Contents: On Lathes, Turning Tools, Turning Wood, Drilling, Screw-cutting, Miscellaneous Apparatus and Processes, Turning particular forms, Staining, Polishing, Spinning Metals, Materials, Ornamental Turning. **300 pages, 99 illustrations, 8vo., cloth. $1.00.***

TURNING LATHES. A guide to Turning, Screw-cutting, Metal-spinning, Ornamental Turning. By JAMES LUKIN. 6th edition. Contents of Chapters: 1. Description of the Lathe. 2. Tools, and How to Use Them. 3. Hard-wood Turning. 4. Metal Turning with Hand Tools. 5. Slide-rest Work in Metal. 6. The Self-acting Lathe. 7. Chuck-making. 8. Turning Articles of Square Section. 9. Screw-cutting by Self-acting Lathe. 10. The Overhead Driving Apparatus. 11. Choosing a Lathe. 12. Grinding and Setting Tools. 13. Metal-spinning. 14. Beddow's (Combined) Epicycloidal, Rose-cutting, Eccentric-cutting, Drilling, Fluting, and Vertical-cutting Appliances. 15. Ornamental Drill and Eccentric Cutter. 16. The Eccentric Chuck. 17. The Dome or Spherical Chuck. 18. The Goniostat. 19. The Oval Chuck. 20. Handy Receipts. **228 pages, illustrated. 12mo., cloth. $1.25.§**

SPIRAL TURNING. An Introduction to Eccentric Spiral Turning, or New Uses for Old Chucks. By H. C. ROBINSON. The Art of Ornamental Turning. Chapter 1. The Spiral Line. 2. The Solid Spiral. 3. Trochoyds. 4. Working the Chucks. 5. The Oval Chuck. 6. Compounding. 7. Geometric Chuck. 8. The Tool-cut. 9. Drawing the Spiral, 10. Cups. With explanation of the plates. **48 pages, 23 illustrations and 12 fine half-tone plates, 8vo., cloth. $2.00.***

Gas and Oil Engines

PRODUCER GAS. The Properties, Manufacture and Uses of Gaseous Fuel, by A. HUMBOLDT SEXTON, F. I. C., F. C. S. The basis of this work was a series of lectures given by the author at the Technical College, Glasgow. Special attention has been given to the principles on which the production of Gaseous Fuel depends. Typical producers have been described including some of the latest forms. The work has been written from a practical man's standpoint and is fully illustrated with sectional drawings. **228 pages, 32 illustrations, 8vo., cloth. $4.00 net.‡**

GAS PRODUCERS for Power Purposes, describing a number of different plants, using various materials for making gas for power purposes. W. A. TOOKEY. 141 pages, with numerous drawings of plants. **Boards. 50 cts.***

PETROL MOTORS Simply Explained. A practical Handbook on the Construction and Working of Petrol Motors, by T. H. HAWLEY. Contents of Chapters: 1. The Principles on which a Petrol Motor Works. 2. The Timing Gear, Valve Action, Cylinder Cooling. 3. The Carburation of Petrol. 4. Ignition Methods. 5. Transmission and Manipulation Gearing; General Arrangement, etc. 6. Hints on Overhauling, and Care of Motor. 7. Maintaining Efficiency. 8. Some Hints on Driving. Index. **99 pages, 19 drawings, 12mo., boards. 50 cts.***

GAS ENGINES, their Advantages, Action and Application, by W. A. TOOKEY. Second edition, revised and enlarged. Part I.—Advantages of a Gas Engine over Electric Motor; Oil Engine; Steam Engine; The Cost of Gas; Up-keep; Attendance; Water; Erection; Powers of Gas Engines; Design of Gas Engines. Part II.—Hints to Buyers; How Gas Engines Work; Notes on the Gas, Air, Water Connections; Hints to Erectors. Part III.—Notes on Starting and Starters; Failures and Defects; Hints to Attendants; Suction Gas Producers. Index. **125 pages, 10 illustrations, 12mo., boards. 50 cts.***

OIL ENGINES, their Selection, Erection and Correction, by W. A. TOOKEY. Second edition. The information in this practical handbook is arranged under the following headings: Part I.—Introductory. Part II.—Selection, Design, Hints to Purchasers. Part III.—Erection, Hints to Erectors. Part IV.—Correction. Appendix.—Various types of Stationary Oil Engines, Portable Oil Engines. **142 pages, 33 illustrations, 12mo., boards. 50 cts.***

The Design and Construction

OF

ÖIL ENGINES.

WITH FULL DIRECTIONS FOR

Erecting, Testing, Installing, Running and Repairing.

Including descriptions of American and English

KEROSENE OIL ENGINES.

By A. H. GOLDINGHAM, M.E.

SYNOPSIS OF CONTENTS OF CHAPTERS:

1. Introductory ; classification of oil engines ; vaporizers ; ignition and spraying devices ; different cycles of valve movements. 2. On design and construction of oil engines ; cylinders ; crankshafts ; connecting rods ; piston and piston rings ; fly-wheels ; air and exhaust cams, valves and valve boxes ; bearings ; valve mechanism, gearing and levers ; proportions of engine frames ; oil-tank and filter ; oil supply pipes ; different types of oil engines ; cylinders made in more than one piece ; single cylinder and double cylinder engines ; crank pin dimensions ; fitting parts ; assembling of oil engine ; testing water jackets, joints, etc. 3. Testing for leaks, faults, power, efficiency, combustion, compression ; defects as shown by indicator ; diagrams for setting valves ; how to correct faults ; indicator fully described ; fuel consumption test, etc. 4. Cooling water tanks ; capacity of tanks ; source of water supply ; system of circulation ; water pump ; exhaust silencers ; self starters ; utilization of waste heat of exhaust. 5. Oil engines driving dynamo ; installation of plant ; direct and belt connected ; belts ; power for electric lighting ; loss of power. 6. Oil engines driving air compressors ; direct connected and geared ; table of pressures ; pumping outfits ; oil engines driving ice and refrigeration outfits. 7. Full instructions for running different kinds of oil engines. 8. Hints on repairs ; adjustment of crank-shaft and connecting rod bearing ; testing oil inlet valves and pump ; fitting new spur gears, etc. 9. General descriptions with illustrations of American and English oil engines ; methods of working ; portable oil engines, etc., etc. Index and tables.

XIII. + 196 pages, 7¼ x 5¼. 79 illustrations, cloth. $2.00

PRACTICAL HANDBOOK

ON

GAS ENGINES.

With Instructions for Care and Working of the Same.

By G. LIECKFELD, C.E.

TRANSLATED WITH PERMISSION OF THE AUTHOR BY

Geo. Richmond, M.E.

TO WHICH HAS BEEN ADDED FULL DIRECTIONS FOR THE RUNNING OF

OIL ENGINES.

CONTENTS.

Choosing and installing a gas engine. The construction of good gas engines. Examination as to workmanship. As to running. As to economy. Reliability and durability of gas engines. Cost of installing a gas engine. Proper erection of a gas engine. Construction of the foundation. Arrangement for gas pipes. Rubber bag. Locking devices. Exhaust pipes. Air pipes. Setting up gas engines. Brakes and their use in ascertaining the power of gas engines. Theory of the brake. The Brauer band brake. Arrangement of a brake test. Explanation of the expressions " Brake Power " and " Indicated Power." Comparisons of the results of the brake test and the indicated test. Quantity of work consumed by external friction of the engine Distribution of heat in a gas engine. Attendance on gas engines. General remarks. Gas engine oil. Cylinder lubricators Rules as to starting and stopping a gas engine. The cleaning of a gas engine. General observations and specific examination for defects. Different kinds of defectives. The engine refuses to work. Non-starting of the engine. Too much pressure on the gas. Water in the exhaust pot. Difficulty in starting the engine. Clogged slide valve. Leaks in gas pipes. Unexpected stopping of engine. Irregular running. Loss of power. Weak gas mixtures. Late ignition. Cracks in air inlet. Back firing. Knocking and pounding inside of engine. Dangers and precautionary measure in handling gas engines. Examination of gas pipes. Precautions when : - Opening gas valves. Removing piston from cylinder. Examining with light openings of gas engines. Dangers in starting Dangers in cleaning. Safeguards for fly-wheels. Danger of putting on belts. **Oil Engines.** Gas engines with producer gas. Gasoline and oil engines The " Hornsby-Akroyd ' oil engine. Failure to start. Examination of engine in detail. Vaporizer valve box. Full detailed directions for the management of Oil Engines. Concluding remarks. 120 pages. Illustrated. 12mo. cloth. $1.00

Dubelle's Famous Formulas.

KNOWN AS

Non Plus Ultra Soda Fountain Requisites of Modern Times

By G. H. DUBELLE.

A practical Receipt Book for Druggists, Chemists, Confectioners and Venders of Soda Water.

SYNOPSIS OF CONTENTS.

INTRODUCTION.—Notes on natural fruit juices and improved methods for their preparation. Selecting the fruit. Washing and pressing the fruit. Treating the juice. Natural fruit syrups and mode of preparation. Simple or stock syrups.

FORMULAS.

FRUIT SYRUPS.—Blackberry, black current, black raspberry, catawba, cherry, concord grape, cranberry, lime, peach, pineapple, plum, quince, raspberry, red current, red orange, scuppernong grape, strawberry; wild grape. NEW IMPROVED ARTIFICIAL FRUIT SYRUPS.—Apple, apricot, banana, bitter orange, blackberry, black current, cherry, citron, curacoa, grape, groseille, lemon, lime, mandarin, mulberry, nectarine, peach, pear, pineapple, plum, quince, raspberry, red current, strawberry, sweet orange, tangerine, vanilla. FANCY SODA FOUNTAIN SYRUPS.—Ambrosia, capillaire, coca-kina, coca-vanilla, coca-vino, excelsior, imperial, kola coca, kola-kina, kola-vanilla, kola-vino, nectar, noyean, orgeat, sherbet, syrup of roses, syrup of violets. ARTIFICIAL FRUIT ESSENCES.—Apple, apricot, banana, bergamot, blackberry, black cherry, black currant, blueberry, citron, cranberry, gooseberry, grape, lemon, lime fruit, melon, nectarine, orange, peach, pear, pineapple, plum, quince, raspberry, red currant, strawberry. CONCENTRATED FRUIT PHOSPHATES. Acid solution of phosphate, strawberry, tangerine, wild cherry.—29 different formulas. NEW MALT PHOSPHATES—36. FOREIGN AND DOMESTIC WINE PHOSPHATES—9. CREAM-FRUIT LACTARTS —28. SOLUBLE FLAVORING EXTRACTS AND ESSENCES—14. NEW MODERN PUNCHES—18. MILK PUNCHES—17. FRUIT PUNCHES—32. FRUIT MEADS—18. NEW FRUIT CHAMPAGNES—17. NEW EGG PHOSPHATES—14. FRUIT JUICE SHAKES —24. EGG PHOSPHATE SHAKES. HOT EGG PHOSPHATE SHAKES. WINE BITTER SHAKES—12. SOLUBLE WINE BITTERS EXTRACTS—12. NEW ITALIAN LEMONADES—18. ICE CREAM SODAS—39. NON-POISONOUS COLORS. FOAM PREPARATIONS. MISCELLANEOUS FORMULAS—26. LATEST NOVELTIES IN SODA FOUNTAIN MIXTURES—7. TONICS.—Beef, iron and cinchona; hypophosphite; beef and coca; beef, wine and iron ; beef, wine, iron and cinchona ; coca and calisaya. LACTARTS. —Imperial tea ; mocha coffee ; nectar; Persian sherbert. PUNCHES. EXTRACTS.—Columbia root beer ; ginger tonic ; soluble hop ale LEMONADES.—French ; Vienna. Egg nogg. Hop ale. Hot tom. Malt wine. Sherry cobbler. Saratoga milk shake. Pancretin and wine. Kola-coco cordial. Iron malt phosphate. Pepsin, wine and iron, etc

157 Pages, Nearly 500 Formulas. 12mo, Cloth, $

MODEL ENGINEER Vol. 7.

How to Become an Electrical Engineer.
How to Make a Lever Switch. Illustrated.
How to Make a Model Battleship. Detail Drawing.
How to Make an Air Compressor, for Driving Model Engines. Detail
   Drawings.
How to set a Simple Slide Valve. Illustrated.
How to Make a Simple Model Steamer. Diagram.
How to Make an Electrical Indicator. Detail Drawings.
How to Make a Model Electric Launch. Detail Drawings.
How to Make a Gramaphone. Detail Drawings.
How to Test Small Engines and Boilers. Diagrams.
How to Make Clock Work Locomotives Detail Drawings.
How to Make a Model Vertical Marine Engine. Detail Drawings.
How to Make a Built-Up Horizontal Steam Engine. Detail Drawings.
How to Make a 40-Ampere-Hour Accumulator. Illustrated.
How to Make a Model Steam Travelling Crane. Detail Drawings.
How to Make a 1 10 H. P. Electric Motor. Detail Drawings.
How to Make a Small Lathe from " Scrap." Illustrated.
How to Make a Power Fretsaw Detail Drawings.
How to Make a Spring Lathe Chuck. Diagrams.
Model " Willians " Central Valve Engine. Detail Drawings.
Two Simp'e Forms of Resistance. Illustrated.
The Motor Bicycle: Its Design, Construction and Use. Many Detail Draw-
   ings.
The Rating of Model Yachts. With Diagrams.
The Stuart Compound Vertical Engine. Complete Detail Drawings.
Construction of Dug out Model Yachts. Detail Drawings.
Construction of 1 2 H. P. Water Motor. Illustrated.
Mr. Taylor's Model Launch Engine. Illustrated
The Pitmaston-Moor-Green Model Railway. Illustrated.
Model Tank Locomotive. Detail Drawings.
Mr Willis' Model Steam Launch. Illustrated.
Original Designs for 750-watt Direct Coupled High Speed Steam Engines.
   and Dynamos with Full Details.
A Four Inch Screw Cutting Lathe. Illustrated
Detail Drawings for 80-watt Multipolar Dynamo.
Design for 100-watt Manchester Type Dynamo.
Model Electric Railway. " Three Rail System," with Diagrams.
Models made without a Lathe. Some Notes on a Large Static Machine.
The Castelli Coherer for Wireless Telegraphy. Illustrated.
A Cheap Petrol Carburetter for Small Gas Engines Illustrated
A Neat Model Electric Launch.
A Water-Regulating Resistance for a 1-in. to 2-in. Spark Coil. Diagrams.
A Carbon Electrolytic Interruptor Illustated.

With many pages of Short Articles, Practical Letters, Notes, Questions and
Answers, Book Notices, Yachting Notes, New Tools, Supplies, &c.

286 pages, 311 Diagrams, 101 Half-Tones, 17 Full Single

Page and Two Double Page Scale Drawings. Bound in Cloth,

Price, **$2.00,** *Net.*

Copies Mailed to any part of the World on Receipt of

Price.

BOOKS ON AERONAUTICS.

RESISTANCE OF AIR AND THE QUESTION OF FLYING. By A. SAMUELSON. An important lecture of considerable interest to those interested in Aeronautics. Contents: Introduction. The Resistance of Plastic Bodies. Air-pressure on Flat Bodies. The Centre of Air-pressure. Distribution of the Air-pressure on the Single Elements of an Inclined Plane. The Normal Air-pressure on a Thin Plane Inclined at an Angle to the Direction of Motion. Lilienthal's Balance of Rotation. The Numerical Value of the Normal Pressure. Flying in General. Flying in Reality. Horizontal Flight by Wing-Flapping. Steering and other Effects of the Stroke. Conclusions. **23 illustrations, 8vo., paper. 75c.‡**

FLIGHT-VELOCITY. By A. SAMUELSON. This work is a short comprehension of extensive scientific investigation and experimental work. Contents: The Rowing Flyer No. 5. The Motor Mechanism. The Fundamental Conditions of Flying by Wing Flapping. The Wings. The Re-sail. Flight Velocity. Living Flyers. Plane or Concave Supporting Surfaces. The False Resolution of Forces. The Erroneous Opinion: the Breadth of an Incline Plane Prevails over its Length. The Centre of Air-pressure, and the Distribution of the Pressure. On the Single Parts of an Inclined Plane. The Principle: the Normal Air-pressure of an Inclined Plane is independent of the Angle of Inclination. Tables of Motion at Varying Angles. The Human Flight. Conclusions. **With five plates, 8vo., paper. 75c.‡**

FLYING MACHINES. Past, Present and Future. A popular account of flying machines, dirigible balloons, By A. W. MARSHALL and H. GREENLY. Whilst the matter in this book is intended as a popular exhibition of the subject, it includes information which will assist the reader with serious intentions of making an attempt to produce a flying machine or air-ship. A great deal of sound experimental work has been done, forming a basis upon which future plans can be calculated. An account of some of this work is here given. Contents of Chapters: 1. Introduction. Dr. Barton's Air-ship. Lebaudy's Military Air-ship. The Deutsch Air-ship. The Wellman Air-ship. Motors of the Wellman Air-ship. Chapter 2. Dirigible Balloons. Giffard's. Dupuy de Lome. Tissandiers'. Krebes'. Santos Dumont's, No. 6 and No. 9. Spencer's Air-ship. Barton's. Maxim's Flying Machine. Archdeacon's Air Propeller Cycle. Barton's, Rawson's, Baulx, Zeppelin, Deutsch, Lambert, Wellman's Air-ships. Trolanini's Air-propelled Boat. Chapter 3. Flying Machines. Giving a Number of those made by Hargrave and also by Phillips, Ader, Maxim, Pilsher's Soaring Wings, Langley, Bastine, Bleirot, Voison, Wright's Gliding Aeroplane, and numerous others. Chapter 4. The Art of Flying. Chapter 5. Flying Machines of the Future. **134 pages, illustrations and page plates, 12mo. 50c.***

EDUCATIONAL WOODWORK. By A. C. HORTH. A complete manual for teachers and organizers of woodworking classes. Contents: 1. First Year Course. 2. Second Year Course. 3. Third Year Course. 4. Fittings and Furniture. 5. Discipline. 6. Organization and Method. 7. The Instruction of the Physically and Mentally Deficient and Blind. 8. Object Lessons. Fully illustrated with photographs, drawings and facsimile blackboard lessons. **159 pages, 12mo., cloth. $1.00.**†

THE BEGINNER'S GUIDE TO CARPENTRY. A practical handbook for Amateurs and Apprentices. By HENRY JARVIS. Contents of Chapters: 1. Indispensable Tools. 2. How to Use the Saw. 3. How to Use the Plane. 4. How to Use Chisels and Gouges. 5. How to Use the Spokeshave, Axe, Pincers, Compasses, Gimlets, Brad-awls, Hammer, etc. 6. Making the Bench. 7. Timber: How Sold, etc. 8. Additional Tools and How to Use Them. 9. Sharpening Tools. 10. Home-made Tools and Appliances. 11. Facing up and Setting out Work. 12. On Setting out and Putting Together Work Joining at Other than Right Angles. 13. Glue: How to Purchase, Prepare, and Use. 14. How to Make Joints: Use of the Plough, etc. 15. Ornamenting Work, Curved Work, Scribing, etc. **128 pages, 99 illustrations, 12mo., boards. 50c.***

MODEL SAILING YACHTS. How to Build, Rig. and Sail Them. A practical handbook for Model Yachtsmen. Edited by PERCIVAL MARSHALL. Contents of Chapters: 1. Introductory: Types of Yachts and Rigs: How to Choose a Model Yacht. 2. The Rating of Model Yachts. 3. The Construction of "Dug-Out" Yachts. 4. The Construction of "Built-Up" Yachts. 5. Sails and Sail Making. 6. Spars and Fittings. 7. Rudders and Steering Gears. 8. Notes on Sailing. **144 pages, 107 illustrations, 12mo., boards. 50c.***

WOODWORK JOINTS. How to make and where to use them; including mortise and tenon joints, lap joints, dovetail joints, glue joints and scarfing joints. With a chapter on Circular Woodwork, revised and enlarged edition. A practical guide for woodworkers. **101 pages, 178 illustrations. 25c.**

THE BEGINNER'S GUIDE TO FRETWORK. Containing full instructions on the Use of Tools and Materials; and six full size fretwork designs. With **39 pages and 26 illustrations. 25c.**

VENEERING, MARQUETRY AND INLAY. A practical instruction book in the art of Decorating Woodwork by these Methods. By P. A. WELLS. **79 pages, 37 illustrations. 25c.**

SOFT WOODS AND COLONIAL TIMBERS. The selection and uses of soft woods and colonial timbers. The cultivation, cutting and seasoning. By P. A. WELLS. **57 pages, 15 illustrations. 25c.**

HARD WOODS, ENGLISH AND FOREIGN. A practical description of hard and fancy woods used by the carpenter and cabinet maker. By P. A. WELLS. **79 pages, 19 illustrations. 25c.**

Spons' Mechanics Own Book

A WORK THAT SHOULD BE IN YOUR BOOKCASE.

The general method of treatment of each subject, is first the raw materials worked upon, its characteristics, variations and suitability; secondly, the tools used, the sharpening and use; thirdly, devoted to typical examples of work to be done, materials, and how to do similar work, etc.

THE FOLLOWING ARE THE PRINCIPAL CONTENTS.

Mechanical Drawing, (13 pages.)
Mechanical Movements, (55 pages.)
Casting and Founding in Brass and Bronze, (30 pages.)
Forging and Finishing, (46 pages.)
Soldering in all its branches, (26 pages.)
Sheet Metal Working, (10 pages.)
Turning and Turning Lathes, (31 pages.)
Carpentry, (224 pages.)
Log Huts, Building, Etc., (8 pages.)
Cabinet-Making, (36 pages.)   Upholstery, (6 pages.)
Carving and Fretwork, (13 pages.)
Picture Frame Making, (4 pages.)
Painting, Graining and Marbling, (28 pages.)
Staining, (13 pages.)   Gilding, (3 pages.)
Polishing, (23 pages.)   Varnishing, (4 pages.)
Paper Hanging, (4 pages.)   Glazing, (7 pages.)
Plastering and White Washing, (9 pages.)
Lighting, (8 pages.)
Foundations and Masonry, (46 pages.)
Roofing, (14 pages.)
Ventilating and Warming, (13 pages.)
Electric Bell and Bell Hanging, Gas Fitting, (8 pages.)
Roads and Bridges, Banks, Hedges, Ditches and Drains, Asphalt Cement Floors, Water Supply and Sanitation.

Total number of pages 702.   Total number illustrations 1,420
Bound in substantial half-extra, - PRICE BY MAIL ONLY $2.50

We have an 8 page circular giving full contents which will be sent free on application.

USEFUL BOOKS.

Picture Frame Making for Amateurs.—Being practical instructions in the making of various kinds of frames, etc. By JAMES LUKIN, B.A. Contents of Chapters:—Necessary tools and materials. Mitred and veneered frames. Round and oval frames. Oxford frames. Bamboo or Japanese work frames. Carved and fretwork frames. Miniature and photograph frames Leatherwork frames. Additional tools and materials. 84 pages, 42 illustrations, 8vo., paper. 40 cts.

Polishes and Stains for Woods—How to use and prepare them. By DAVID DENNING. Contents of Chapters:—Introductory. General remarks on polishing. French polishing and bodying in. Spiriting off in French polishing. Glazing as a means of finishing. The workroom and its fittings. Fillers for wood to be French polished. Wax polishing. Oil polishing. Dry shining and polishing turned work, fretwork, marquetry and inlaid work. Staining and darkening woods. Ebonizing woods and dull polishing. Preparation of polishes. Preparation of stains. 70 pages, 8vo, paper. 40 cts.

Wood Carving for Amateurs.—Containing descriptions of all the requisite tools and full instructions for their use. By D. DENNING. Contents of Chapters:—Preliminary. Tools. Wood. Bench and methods of holding work. Sharpening tools. Panel carving. Various examples for carving. Chip-carving. Antique carving. Index. 84 pages, 56 illustrations and 8 folding plates, 12mo., paper. 40 cts.

French Polishers Manual, by a French Polisher. A practical guide. Contents:—Wood staining; washing; matching; improving; painting; imitation; directions for staining; sizing and embodying; smoothing; spirit varnishing; French polishing; directions for repolishing; general remarks and useful receipts. 31 pages, 16mo., paper. 20 cts.

Bookbinding for Amateurs, being descriptions of the various tools and appliances required and minute instructions for their effective use. By W. J. E. CRANE. Contents of Chapters: 1. Introductory. 2. Tools and appliances. 3 Materials. 4. Folding. 5. Placing plates, beating and pressing books. 6. Sawing and sewing. 7. Affixing end papers, rounding and backing. 8. Getting into boards. 9 Cutting and bevelling in boards. 10. Coloring edges. 11. Gilding edges. 12. Materials for marbling edges. 13. Marbling edges or paper. 14. Headbands and registers. 15. Lining the back. 16. Covering 17. Marbling and coloring leather. 18. Pain finishing. 19. Half and full gilt finishing. 20. Antique and monastic finishing. 21. Whole bound finishing. 22. Conclusion. Index. 184 pages, 156 illustrations, 12mo, cloth. $1.00.

Artistic Amusements, being instructions for a variety of art work for home employment, and suggestions for novel and saleable articles for fancy bazaars. Index. 113 pages, illus., cloth, $1.00.

PAINT AND COLOR MIXING.

A Practical Handbook

For Painters, Decorators, and all Who Have to Mix Colors.

Containing many samples of Oil and Water Paints of various colors, including the principal Graining Grounds, and upwards of 500 different Color Mixtures, with Hints on Color and Paint Mixing generally. Testing Colors, Receipts for Special Paints, &c., &c.

By ARTHUR SEYMOUR JENNINGS.

Second Edition, Rewritten and Considerably Enlarged.

CONTENTS OF CHAPTERS.

I.—Paint and Color Mixing.
II.—Colors or Strainers.
III.—Reds and How to Mix Them.
IV.—Blues and How to Mix Them.
V.—Yellows and How to Mix Them.
VI.—Greens and How to Mix Them.
VII.—Browns and How to Mix Them.
VIII.—Greys and How to Mix them.
IX.—Whites and How to Mix Them.
X.—Black Japan in Color Mixing.
XI.—Graining Grounds and Graining Colors.
XII.—Water Paints, Painting and Varnishing over Water Paints, Distempers, &c.
XIII.—Testing Colors, Purity of Materials, Tone, Fineness of Grinding, Spreading Capacity, &c.
XIV.—Notes on Color Harmony.
XV.—Tables, Notes and Receipts, Care of Brushes, Putty Receipts, &c. Description of Colored Plates. Index.

The eight plates contain 171 samples of Colors, Graining Grounds, Tints of Water Paints, and Non=Poisonous Distempers.

This is the most Practical and Up=to=Date Work on this Subject, is very clearly written, and will enable any man who studies it to make Bigger Wages.

With 149 pages of descriptive matter, 8vo, cloth, price, $2.50

Lightning Source UK Ltd.
Milton Keynes UK
UKHW02f0406030518
322021UK00006B/775/P